IRISH RAILWAY RAMBLER

THE RAILWAY PHOTOGRAPHS
OF MICHAEL McMAHON

COLOURPOINT

Published 2015 by Colourpoint Books
an imprint of Colourpoint Creative Ltd
Colourpoint House, Jubilee Business Park
21 Jubilee Road, Newtownards, BT23 4YH
Tel: 028 9182 6339
Fax: 028 9182 1900
E-mail: info@colourpoint.co.uk
Web: www.colourpoint.co.uk

First Edition
First Impression

A catalogue record for this book is available from the British Library.

Designed by April Sky Design, Newtownards
Tel: 028 9182 7195
Web: www.aprilsky.co.uk

Printed by W&G Baird Ltd, Antrim

ISBN 978-1-78073-075-2

CONTENTS

INTRODUCTION

This personal memoir recalls nearly forty years during which most of my spare time was devoted to observing and photographing the railways of Ireland. I started my photography in 1975, helped by the extensive use of my school darkroom in Co Tyrone, and until 1982, images were a mix of black and white and colour film prints. Thereafter I worked solely with colour slides until this mode finally yielded to the digital era. I was very likely one of the last railway photographers exclusively working with colour transparencies, until I withdrew from railway photography.

There were three main phases of diesel power on the railways of Ireland:

1. Early individual pioneer railcars, a mix of small classes of locomotives, and quite successful fleets of railcar sets from AEC, BUT, the UTA developing MEDs and MPDs.
2. Larger fleets of locomotives, from Sulzer, Metropolitan-Vickers and of course General Motors, NIR used their 70 and 80 classes to full advantage.
3. Limited use of locomotives in push-pull formations, and a resurgence of the railcar from Alsthom, CAF, Rotem.

My period of photography mainly coincided with the mid-phase as described above, and for that reason earlier classes are not included in this work, even though a few stragglers of Sulzers, and E Class shunters were still around, but mostly during my black and white days.

In many ways my withdrawal from railway photography was appropriate. I was fortunate to enjoy the last of the 'museum years' of the railway network typified by traditional locomotives and carriages, mechanical signalling, steam heating, travelling post offices and freight trains. In those days many of the station buildings and other structures remained intact and virtually unchanged from the days of steam. Picturesque though Córas Iompair Éireann was, the museum atmosphere was directly related to financial circumstance, there being an official reluctance to inject overdue capital for modernisation. A spate of derailments and other accidents brought belated Governmental recognition that under-investment was both a false and a dangerous economy. The investment that followed changed the character of the system with modern signalling, much simplified track layouts, new rolling stock and to widespread regret, the advance of the bus-shelter school of railway architecture – on both sides of the Border.

These changes were paralleled by the encroachment of health and safety regulations that have restricted the enthusiasts' means of access to the railway, most importantly and rightly with regard to trespass. Study of a number of views in this work will reveal that they were only possible by 'being inside the fence' so a word of explanation is warranted. Early photography was limited to stations and the line-side, until I started to use the Rail Runabout, Rambler and Rover tickets. The use of a 'big' ticket at least twice a year to an extent far beyond anything that CIÉ could have imagined was thoroughly enjoyable, but gruelling. All I needed after every ticket was a good rest!

The scope and diversity of my railway photography changed immeasurably through involvement in railway societies. Serving initially on the operations committee of the Railway Preservation Society of Ireland, I later became Operations Officer (Northern), as well as Chairman of The Modern Railway Society of Ireland. Both organisations promote rail tours throughout the island of Ireland with both steam and diesel power. The time-consuming management of these events demanded close liaison and harmonious relations with railway personnel in different technical disciplines, and at varying seniority levels. The enthusiasm of the Societies' officers to make these events a success was complemented

by high levels of help and commitment extended by professional railwaymen. They were anxious to promote their railways, and on many occasions, we were treated almost like members of staff.

Working with the professionals in this fashion led to a footplate pass that allowed access well beyond anything possible with a Rambler or Rover ticket. The ability to travel everywhere that enjoyed a train service, be it passenger, freight or mails, was a privilege that I exploited to the full by covering an estimated 80,000 miles on the footplate between 1982 and 1995. In the process I met and made friends with innumerable railwaymen at stations, on trains and in signal cabins, exchanging news and views, and listening to stories from times past. A particularly cherished memory arose from talking to sorters on the mail trains, requesting nice clear postmarks for slide films and letters I was posting in the Travelling Post Office (TPO). Eventually I was invited aboard one night and travelled with them as they sorted mail between Moate and Mullingar.

The texture of the railway has changed beyond recognition during the years surveyed in this work, but the character and stature of railwaymen has not. I hope that many of those that I met on my travels as well as the railway enthusiast community at large will enjoy the result.

* * *

Selection of suitable images from a very large collection was a lengthy task. My preference has always been to record the unusual as well as the normal scene of railway men going about their normal duties, and I hope that this mixture is suitably reflected. Writing the captions and checking their contents took even longer, but it provided immense enjoyment in learning so much more about the circumstances and background to what is depicted. There are many more pictures to publish. While this work features mainly rolling stock and equipment, possible topics for a further book could include freight, cross-border, mail trains, cement, night photography and beet to name just a few. Thanks are due to Charles Friel, who willingly undertook the thankless task of proof-reading, and friends, Alan McFerran and William Watson for their help and suggestions. The Journals of the Irish Railway Record Society and The Irish Traction Group, as well as The Irish Railfans News, proved essential for checking details. Any residual errors are entirely of my own making.

Finally I must acknowledge that the pictures in this work would have lain in the files, perhaps only to be aired at meetings of like-minded enthusiasts, but for one man. Norman Johnston of Colourpoint pleaded for an Irish Diesel album, but there were always so many other things to do that this project sat on the long finger for several years. A great debt is owed to Norman for his dedication to the cause of Irish railway publishing, which has left the enthusiast community significantly better served and informed. It is a sadness that he is no longer with us to see these results of his dogged persistence.

Michael McMahon
October 2015

A Class

The determination of the Board of Córas Iompair Éireann to rapidly eliminate steam traction led to the widely-publicised signing of a contract for 60 Co-Co Class A and 34 Bo-Bo Class C locomotives in May 1954. At the time, this was the largest ever export order placed for British-built diesel-electric locomotives. It was common knowledge that General Motors and other US manufacturers had considerable experience with their proven, competent designs. However for several reasons, not least shortage of foreign currency reserves, a tender submitted by a consortium of four British manufacturers was preferred. The consortium partners were Crossley for diesel engines; Metropolitan-Cammell Carriage & Wagon Co for mechanical parts; Metropolitan-Vickers for electrical equipment; English Steel Corporation for body structure.

No A1, the first of 60 silver liveried Co-Co Class A locomotives, arrived in Dublin in July 1955, heralding the dawn of a new age. The Class leader was in traffic by the end of September and initial performance was good although braking techniques were difficult to master, leading to the fitting of driver's vigilance equipment. Unfortunately the smoky, noisy, oily Crossley engines soon proved unreliable with unacceptably high failure rates that could not be redressed despite the best efforts of Inchicore staff.

Introduction of Class 121 in 1961 cogently demonstrated the comparative superiority of the General Motors power plant, but tough negotiations were necessary before GM could be persuaded to sell engines only, which was contrary to their standard policy of producing complete locomotives only. Two Class C locomotives (C233 and C234) were experimentally fitted with Maybach MD-650 1200 hp engines in 1965 and although these units were difficult to maintain, the exercise proved the commercial feasibility of an engine replacement programme.

GM eventually relented and provided two of their 645-E engines that were fitted to Nos A58/59 in mid 1968. So positive were the results that the entire class had been re-engined with GM units by late 1971. For front line express services with speeds up to 80 mph, eight (Nos A2/27/35/36/46/54/56/59) had their engines up-rated to 1650 hp; most were later converted back to 1200 hp in conformity with the remainder. Even with the introduction of Class 071 in 1976, Class A haulage of passenger trains remained commonplace. Footplate travel at 75 mph with a nice set of Cravens coaches on a limited stopping train on the Cork mainline was a most pleasant experience.

The driver of No 054 watches loading of gypsum at Kingscourt as an interested local man approaches the locomotive on Monday 7 May 1984. This locomotive had worked the empty wagons from Drogheda at 05.30, arriving at 08.00. Departure was timetabled for 10.45 but generally the train left earlier as soon as it was loaded.

Note the staff exchange 'snatcher arm' still fitted on the cab side. This was once lowered manually by a 'Snatcherman' to exchange the miniature single line staff from lineside equipment. These arms remained on some locomotives long after the use of this equipment had ceased; some of Class 071 were so equipped from new despite the last use of mechanical ETS exchange ceasing on the Sligo line in June 1982. Inside the cab there was always a draught around knee height where the chain passed through the bodyside. Weekly circulars were useful for plugging this hole until they became soggy and fell out.

A truck used to transport gypsum from the nearby mine can be seen in the background and, if there was no train, it would be stockpiled in the shed on the left. Kingscourt yard was dusty in dry weather but when it rained, it was extremely mucky and the pink-coloured gypsum stuck to shoes like glue.

No 051 gingerly crosses a 'crow's nest' of sleepers at the bomb-damaged O'Rourke's Bridge (bridge No 164) with a special train of empty fertiliser and cement wagons from Adelaide Yard on Wednesday 3 October 1984. The bridge had been damaged in an explosion during the evening of 29 September but the experienced repair gangs had the down line reopened by noon three days later. NIR had undertaken extensive work over the previous few years in replacement of underbridge arches with flat concrete spans supported by strong cross beams, which enabled repairs to be completed much faster.

The mountain in the background is Slieve Gullion; the fields above the rear of No 051's train are on the lower slopes of the mountain below the trees of the Slieve Gullion Forest Park.

The Moy River bridge at milepost 156 on the Ballina branch is the location for this photograph of No 030 working the 15.40 Ballina–Dublin via Mullingar on Sunday 14 October 1984. Due into Connolly at 20.15, a four and a half hour journey in a rattly, noisy and under-heated Park Royal coach was not to be relished.

When the new Athlone 'Southern' station opened in January 1985, the 15.40 continued to call despite having to reverse to regain the former MGWR line towards Mullingar. From January 1986, the train was retimed to 15.35 and ran via Portarlington to Dublin Heuston. The flimsy Moy Bridge built in 1860 was upgraded in November 1996, thereby finally allowing Classes 071 and 201 to reach Ballina.

The laden ammonia train from Marino Point on the Cobh branch to Shelton Abbey near Arklow, hauled by No 021, is illuminated by a red signal beside the signal cabin at Cork on Thursday 30 January 1986. The scheduled departure time for this important train was 14.45 from Marino Point. It was the last and slowest in a procession of four timetabled trains, the preceding services being the 14.45 Cork–Dublin Heuston passenger service, the 15.00 Cork–Tralee passenger service, and the 15.10 up Day Mail Cork–Dublin Heuston. The ammonia train was timetabled to run non-stop to Dublin Connolly (arriving 19.42) for a crew change, although it was often 'looped' to allow other trains to overtake. A prolonged industrial relations dispute at the Shelton Abbey fertilizer factory between 22 October and 10 December 1985 had dislocated timetabled traffic flows and it took time for the plant to return to regular production. On this occasion the train was much delayed, running in a Saturdays only 20.20 path, arriving in Dublin Connolly at 01.25 the following morning for the crew change, and arrival at Shelton Abbey Siding was at 03.20. The sorters are busy in the Travelling Post Office (TPO) on the left preparing for that evening's 21.30 up Night Mail.

No 058 passes the signal cabin at Castletown between Athlone and Mullingar on Sunday 12 July 1987 with the 15.30 Ballina–Dublin Connolly. The GAA Munster Hurling Final was being played that day at Thurles, requiring eight special trains from Cork, two from Dublin Heuston and one

each from Mallow, Limerick and Charleville. These extra movements placed considerable strain on the coaching stock roster, resulting in the use of Park Royal coaching stock on the 15.30. Due to operating restrictions, this stock could not work via Portarlington and the train was diverted to Dublin Connolly. A substitute bus left Roscommon at 17.10 to run to Dublin calling at Athlone and the other stations usually served by this train.

As an indication of the intense traffic movements elsewhere that Sunday, David Bowie had been playing in concert at Slane requiring a special from Dublin Heuston to Cork. Also Killaloe parish organised a Knock Special to Claremorris from Ballybrophy via Nenagh, Limerick and Gort, and the GAA Connaught Football Final at Castlebar required a special working. NIR operated CIÉ's share of the Belfast–Dublin services on this day to release sufficient stock for the specials.

No 027 shunts to the rear of the 15.15 Cork–Tralee at Mallow during the blue paint phase on Tuesday 4 August 1987. The train at the bay platform is the delayed 15.05 Cork to Dublin up Day Mail hauled by 129 which was having locomotive problems. The Class 141 on the far end of the 15.15 set hauled the train to Mallow, and later shunted the yard on the left. No 027 had been idling in the bay platform since early morning, and would later work the continuation of the 15.15 ex-Cork to Tralee and would return that evening to Mallow with the 18.25 Liner-Mail.

No 053 is in the running shed at Dublin Connolly on Saturday 12 September 1987 together with No 173. Both locomotive numbers have the 'S' suffix meaning that the in-cab audible warning signalling system (CAWS) has been fitted. No 053 entered traffic in June 1956 and received its up-rated engine in August 1971. It was stopped in December 1992, formally withdrawn in March 1995, and cut up at Inchicore in May 1995.

Class leader No 001 at the end of the line at Rosslare Harbour Pier after arrival with the 13.35 from Dublin Connolly on Saturday 11 June 1988. The Pier station was still virtually intact at this stage with accommodation for Customs Inspection, a booking office, inspectors and staff offices, and the traditional CIÉ buffet-bar. It was a pleasant place in good weather to spend a few hours, waiting for the next boat to arrive. On a stormy night, the breaking spray from waves crashing onto the harbour wall would soak any coaching stock stabled there making it essential to keep doors and windows closed!

On the same day, No 001 has run round its train and the shunter has coupled up the stock. The train has moved off the pier to the platform called 'Rosslare Harbour Mainland'. There remained only the brake test to perform before departing at 18.00 for Dublin Connolly. Ballygeary signal cabin on the right was destroyed by fire on 15 December 1997, and was eventually replaced with a ground frame recovered from the Abbey sidings at Waterford.

The concrete bridge to the right was one of the earliest concrete bridges in Ireland and was constructed in 1904/5 by McAlpine along with many others for the opening of the line between Rosslare and Waterford.

The entire track pictured here was taken out of use in April 2008. The Europort station was replaced by a bus shelter to the right, nearer to the town, from where most of the traffic now originates.

No 029SA is in charge of a crane special for bridge replacement duties at Knockcroghery on Tuesday 14 June 1988. This remote underbridge near milepost 92 required the two ex-BR Cowans & Sheldon thirty ton steam cranes of 1960-vintage purchased in 1973 and re-gauged at Inchicore. The cranes were withdrawn in March 2001, and cut up at Inchicore in August 2009.

Regarding No 029's 'SA' suffix, 'S' denotes installation of in-cab audible signalling warning system and, uniquely for this class, the 'A' suffix denotes air brakes. When air-braked, this locomotive could be seen working shale trains between Kilmastulla and Castlemungret. The trial to fit air brakes to the class generally did not extend beyond No 029. Indeed this engine had less than a month's service left when this picture was taken; it was stopped on 13 July 1988, but not scrapped for almost six years.

No 036 crosses from the down main and approaches the flat crossing at Limerick Junction with the 08.20 (Saturdays only) Dublin Heuston–Cork on Saturday 30 July 1988. The Cork main line timetable for this weekend had been substantially revised to accommodate the huge number of concert goers travelling to see Michael Jackson in concert at Cork. The specials started arriving in Cork on the Friday morning and the last of the concert goers did not leave until the Monday afternoon; a very intense bank holiday weekend for Irish Rail staff in Cork.

Cork shed contains some interesting residents on the evening of Sunday 31 July 1988. The on-loan NIR railcars are scheduled to work on Cobh services. The steam crane is ex-BR, one of two purchased in June 1973 and is protected from the elements. Nos 159 and 027 stand idle awaiting their next duties.

The Class A cabs were draughty with the often ill-fitting droplight windows stuffed around the edges with newspapers to improve matters. The best cab heater was the hotplate at ankle level on the passenger side, which was always left on, thereby warming the entire centre console. An attempt was made to improve the window fit as with No 025 in the 'ramps shop' at Inchicore on Saturday 16 September 1989. Only Nos 025 and 053 were so treated as within a few years, large scale withdrawals commenced. No 025 was stopped in August 1993.

Beauparc in the evening light as No 051 restarts the empty Tara mines train across the train guard-operated level crossing on Monday 12 February 1990. This train had left the Alexander Road terminal in Dublin's docklands at 15.05, and was due at the mine near Navan at 17.30. Reloading took two hours and the train then worked back as far as Drogheda for stabling overnight before continuing to Dublin at 04.50 the following morning.

Note the aluminium gutter fitted across the footplate windows. This was an attempt to divert the oil in the engine exhaust from smearing the glass, especially in rain when it became a translucent smudge.

Freshly out-shopped, No 022 gleams on oily track at the running shed at Inchicore on Sunday 25 February 1990. Unfortunately it did not remain in service for much longer as it was stopped with a cracked wheel in early 1992. A decision on its future was deferred and then cancelled in December 1992 together with approximately seventeen others of the rapidly-diminishing class.

This example was formally withdrawn in November 1994 and cut up at Inchicore in March 1995.

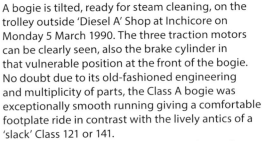

A bogie is tilted, ready for steam cleaning, on the trolley outside 'Diesel A' Shop at Inchicore on Monday 5 March 1990. The three traction motors can be clearly seen, also the brake cylinder in that vulnerable position at the front of the bogie. No doubt due to its old-fashioned engineering and multiplicity of parts, the Class A bogie was exceptionally smooth running giving a comfortable footplate ride in contrast with the lively antics of a 'slack' Class 121 or 141.

No 019 in the background was at Inchicore for minor attention and remained in service until, during a planned engine replacement in mid-1993, it was discovered that the electrical wiring was sub-standard. Despite cab refurbishment and a repaint, it was stopped in June 1993, formally withdrawn in March 1995, and scrapped at Inchicore in May 1995.

The 15.15 Waterford–Dublin Heuston headed by No 081 is ready to start its journey on Wednesday 13 June 1990 as No 005 idles in the bay platform. The short train of Park Royal coaches and a 'Dutch van'

headed by 005 had arrived earlier in the morning at 08.27 with the 07.15 from Rosslare Harbour. It stood there until returning with the 17.00, and then formed the 19.40 Rosslare Harbour–Limerick – hardly an intensive roster!

Inside the paint shop at Inchicore, No 021 has just been sprayed almost all over orange on Thursday 13 September 1990. With the paint not fully hardened, the locomotive was shunted to a nearby shed for the application of white stripes, logos and minor detail finishing. No 021's return to service did not last long as traction motor problems in June 1992 led to withdrawal the following November and scrapping at Inchicore in June 1994.

The staggered platforms at Fota on the Cork to Cobh branch provide the setting for No 047 working a larger than usual set of Cravens coaches on the 18.20 from Cobh to Cork on Saturday 15 June 1991. The following day, the GAA Munster Football Semi-Finals were played at Killarney and this set would be used for one of the three specials. No 047 was the last of the remaining class members to receive the white stripe treatment, receiving it around September 1993. It was not destined to wear it for long as withdrawal took place in mid-November because of generator and traction motor faults.

The Royal Canal looks reasonably clear as No 019 on the 17.05 Dublin Connolly–Sligo passes Croke Park Stadium on Friday 21 June 1991. This well-supported train operated to Sligo on Fridays only; for the rest of the week it departed at 17.15 and ran to Mullingar only, returning from there at 20.10. The set off the

17.05 (Fridays only) remained at Sligo until working the 04.50 the following Monday morning unless required for weekend specials. Then, it would work back empty from Sligo late on Friday evening, returning to Sligo in time to form the 'Early Bird' on Monday morning.

A sad line up, mainly consisting of Class A locomotives outside the ramps shop at Inchicore on a grey Wednesday 1 July 1992. Left to right are Nos 031/038/033/161/027/016/039 and 007. Some look quite fresh; the decision to stop work was usually taken while they were going through the workshops. A few locomotives would hang around for some time awaiting a final decision. For example No 027 had been stopped the previous month but was not formally withdrawn until November 1994, but was then cut up quite quickly in March 1995.

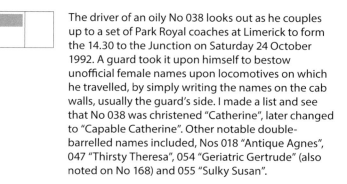

The driver of an oily No 038 looks out as he couples up to a set of Park Royal coaches at Limerick to form the 14.30 to the Junction on Saturday 24 October 1992. A guard took it upon himself to bestow unofficial female names upon locomotives on which he travelled, by simply writing the names on the cab walls, usually the guard's side. I made a list and see that No 038 was christened "Catherine", later changed to "Capable Catherine". Other notable double-barrelled names included, Nos 018 "Antique Agnes", 047 "Thirsty Theresa", 054 "Geriatric Gertrude" (also noted on No 168) and 055 "Sulky Susan".

This was a shock when I first saw it as No 019 had become the guinea pig in livery trials for the new Class 201 then on order and is pictured here at the ramps shop at Inchicore on Friday 13 May 1994. The livery is similar to that finally applied to the 201s, although still under consideration around the cab roof and front where the masking tape is still in position. No 019 was selected for the trial as it had been recently painted but its overhaul had been suddenly cancelled. The locomotive therefore had a smooth paint-ready surface.

The 201s when delivered had black window wipers and cab window surrounds, but did not carry the Irish Rail Logo. The new Iarnrod Éireann three pin plug-like branding was launched to coincide with the formal handing over of No 201 at Inchicore in June 1994.

121 Class

In 1955–1957, CIÉ was persuaded for a variety of reasons to purchase diesel locomotives from Birmingham Railway and Carriage Works/Sulzer locomotives, plus Classes A and C from Metropolitan Vickers, notwithstanding the widely-accepted quality of General Motors' products. The need to dieselise further services led to an order with General Motors in mid-1960 for fifteen of their type GL8 (G = single cab, L = lightweight, 8 = 8 cylinder 567 CR engine at 950 hp). This was GM's first European export order, and they were classic American hood style Bo-Bo 'switchers', fitted with a single brake block to each wheel and also sanding equipment!

Numbered B121–B135, they entered traffic between February and April 1961 and performed well. There were initial reservations about driver sighting when running bonnet-first, and also their brake power when working loose-coupled goods trains. The bonnet-first problem was initially solved by working with the cab leading, necessitating retention of turntables for many years. Multiple working equipment was installed during the early 1970s which allowed their coupling in pairs, bonnet to bonnet. The sanding equipment was eventually removed in the early 1970s having been long out of use.

Class 121 entered service to replace steam engines. Compared to today's soundproofed, ergonomically designed and computer assisted locomotives and railcars, they were quite modern for their time and gave almost forty years of reliable service.

No 126 is turned at Youghal after arriving with the Irish Railway Record Society Special from Cork on Saturday 6 July 1985. The Special departed Cork at 12.45, arriving at Youghal at 14.00 after stops at Carrigtwohill and Mogeely. The return working departed at 17.00, stopping at Killeagh and Cobh Junction, and arrived back in Cork at 18.15. In this view, local children greatly outnumber the Special's passengers – and also the footplate crew.

Two coaches from the Great Southern Railway Preservation Society at Mallow were attached to the six CIÉ Cravens coaches in Cork, making a total of eight coaches and two vans; quite a load for a single 121! Repairs to the turntable decking by the works and buildings department are evident. It had been some years since the table was last used. This Special train was organised by the Cork area of the Irish Railway Record Society as part of the anniversary celebrations for 'Cork 800'.

Snow lies at Sligo, and the platform starting signal is off as Nos 130 and 132 prepare to start the 18.00 to Dublin Connolly on Wednesday 29 January 1986. The cab of a 121 on a frosty night was a pleasant place to be with warm air draughts coming through holes in the centre driving console. These engines were fitted with cooking facilities for the crew and the glow of the hotplate helped to top up the heat!

Nos 134 and 135 stand near the site of the former Waterford and Limerick's loco shed in the Sallypark yard, Waterford, on a sunny afternoon on Tuesday 8 July 1986. They had arrived earlier in the day with the 13.15 Bell Ferry liner service from Dublin Heuston.

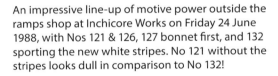

An impressive line-up of motive power outside the ramps shop at Inchicore Works on Friday 24 June 1988, with Nos 121 & 126, 127 bonnet first, and 132 sporting the new white stripes. No 121 without the stripes looks dull in comparison to No 132!

Belfast City Hospital halt, Nos 122 and 129 pass with the 10.30 from Dublin Connolly to Belfast Central on Sunday 24 July 1988. This very unusual motive power for the Enterprise was organised by the Great Southern Railway Preservation Society. It was more than twenty years since a pair of 121s had been seen on a cross-border passenger working. Also, this was the first occasion that they had visited Belfast Central, apart from the previous day's clearance trial with Nos 122 and 135. Then, everyone held their breaths in traversing the narrow bores of the bridges under the Donegall and Ormeau Roads, but the paint was not even scraped! The 121s returned to Dublin later in the afternoon on the 15.00 from Belfast Central.

No 124 sports the (thankfully) short-lived green stripe livery at Dublin Connolly on Wednesday 8 February 1989. One coach from a push-pull set was also painted with a green stripe but that lasted even less time. The green was similar to that applied to the DART sets so perhaps the intention was a hybrid 'Suburban' livery.

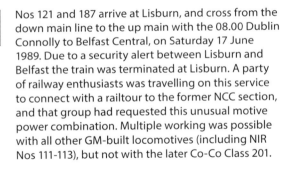

Nos 121 and 187 arrive at Lisburn, and cross from the down main line to the up main with the 08.00 Dublin Connolly to Belfast Central, on Saturday 17 June 1989. Due to a security alert between Lisburn and Belfast the train was terminated at Lisburn. A party of railway enthusiasts was travelling on this service to connect with a railtour to the former NCC section, and that group had requested this unusual motive power combination. Multiple working was possible with all other GM-built locomotives (including NIR Nos 111-113), but not with the later Co-Co Class 201.

Bonnet-first working of 121s was rare. Here is No 129 waiting at Clara with a failed push-pull set on a wintry Sunday 25 February 1990 while No 086 overtakes on the 09.05 from Galway. The vertical white line on the former goods store wall on the right was the driver's marker to ensure that the rear of a Mark 3 train had the guard's van doors adjacent to the short platform.

Pairs of 121s working passenger trains on the Waterford line were also fairly rare. Here, Nos 127 and 129 with a rake of Mark 2 coaches are about to depart the Crystal City with the 18.20 to Dublin Heuston on Monday 11 June 1990. These two locomotives were, unusually, paired together continuously between April and July 1990.

At the Dublin end of Cork station, both locomotives are the first of their respective classes. No 121 is working the 15.00 Day Mail to Dublin Heuston, while No 141 has charge of the 15.15 to Tralee, on Friday 15 June 1990. Unusually No 141 has the Irish Rail logo on a panel that appears to have been placed on top of the CIÉ roundel on the front of the locomotive; the black paint of the panel is cleaner!

No 121 was the last operational class member to receive the white stripe treatment in April 1990. The only example not to acquire this decoration was damaged No 125 which was stored out of use at Inchicore following a fire in March 1986.

Nos 131 and 135 are at Mostrim with the 13.20 from Dublin Connolly–Sligo on Monday 22 June 1992 waiting to cross Nos 168 and 151 on the 13.20 from Sligo. Although it clearly says 'Edgeworthstown' on

the signal cabin, Irish Rail referred to the station as 'Mostrim' on timetables, tickets and even the Electric Train Staff! Local agitation about the confusion led Irish Rail to revert to the use of Edgeworthstown only from June 1996.

Class 121 performed regularly on the Sligo line until a spate of bad failures around Christmas 1989 saw them replaced by a batch of selected members of Classes 141/181. Those so favoured were replaced by Class 071 in October 1993, and then reliability really improved.

No 132 is pictured at Charleville while working the 15.00 up Day Mail from Cork to Dublin Heuston on Monday 29 June 1992. The single coach passenger accommodation with this service was withdrawn on introduction of the new mainline timetable from 18 May 1992.

Driver and guard push No 121 round at Mullingar on Wednesday 1 July 1992, having arrived with the 17.15 from Dublin Connolly. This train comprised four Cravens carriages and a 'Dutch van' rather than the usual push-pull set, necessitating the engine to be turned for the return 20.10 working. A single Class 141 was usually rostered for these duties, which meant a simple run round rather than a spin on the turntable.

On Saturday 17 July 1993 No 127 sports one of each of the two types of battery tail-lamps at Drogheda, while awaiting departure with the 17.07 to Dublin Pearse, stopping at all stations to Howth Junction except Gormanston and Portmarnock.

No 049 is stabled on the middle road with the cable plough train. Re-signalling work then in progress between Drogheda and Malahide was completed in May 1994. Initially controlled from Drogheda, CTC in Dublin took over in July 1994. On the extreme left beyond the fence, a gypsum hopper wagon can be seen, loaded with ballast. That area, known as 'Buckies Sidings' would later become the €42 million railcar depot, which opened in late 2003.

Derby Day at the Curragh on Sunday 26 June 1994 saw two NIR specials from Belfast Central. The first, departing at 09.00 was hauled by NIR No 112 Northern Counties throughout. The second, departing at 09.30, had a locomotive change at Dublin Connolly. Nos 131 and 133 worked the train from there to the Curragh, running as empty carriages to Kildare and back to Dublin Heuston for stabling. Here we can see this pair near Cherryville Junction rushing the 16.30 empty carriages from Heuston to Portarlington. Kildare station was busy with race traffic as well as regular traffic; it was easier to run round the NIR set and stable at Portarlington instead. The empty carriages left Portarlington at 18.25, collecting the passengers at the Curragh at 18.55, arriving at Belfast Central at 22.00.

In this picture for the modellers, No 124 is well 'hemmed in' at the former Enniskillen bay platform in Dundalk on Sunday 19 March 1995. Introduced to traffic in March 1961, this engine was withdrawn in June 2008 with wheels down to scrap size. It is now preserved by the Irish Traction Group at Moyasta Junction, Co Clare, having moved there from Inchicore in November 2009.

On the afternoon of Saturday 6 June 1998, Nos 131 and 124 bask in the sun at Waterford during a break in the Irish Railway Record Society railtour from Dublin Connolly to Rosslare, Waterford and return via Lavistown Loop. This train comprised the Mark 3 Executive set; the other coaches in this photograph formed that evening's 17.00 to Rosslare Europort. In spite of its smart appearance, No 131 would suffer a serious bogie fire at Limerick Junction on 18 December 2001, leading to formal withdrawal in February 2003 and scrapping at Inchicore in March 2003.

141 and 181 Classes

The success of Class 121 introduced in 1961 gave General Motors a firm foothold in Ireland, placing that manufacturer in a strong position to bid for the remaining diesel locomotives needed finally to eliminate steam. Fast delivery times and established reputation for reliability clinched the deal and thirty-seven locomotives were ordered in May 1962. The GM type designation was JL8 (J = dual cabbed, L = lightweight, 8 = 8 cylinder 567 CR engine at 950 hp); their road numbers were B141 to B177. Designed specially for CIÉ, they were essentially a double-cabbed version of Class 121. Shipment was effected between November 1962 and January 1963, the first locomotive starting service on 10 December 1962.

While the first batch successfully accounted for the remaining steam fleet, more were needed to replace ageing AEC railcars, and an order was issued for twelve GM type JL18 locomotives in 1966. Externally similar to Class 141, the engine was of the 8-645 E type giving 1100 hp, compared to 950 hp from the earlier 8-567CR engine. This later batch, numbered B181 to B192, was delivered in late 1966.

Classes 141 and 181, as they later became, were fitted with two brake blocks per wheel and multiple working equipment. Class 121 was later retro-fitted with this equipment enabling all three types to work in multiple. For rostering purposes little distinction was drawn between the classes except in later days.

The sad remains of No 145 at Dundalk North on Friday 7 December 1984. It had been hijacked at O'Rourke's Bridge in South Armagh while working the 16.55 Dundalk–Adelaide (12.45 from Dublin Heuston)–Guinness Liner train on 3 December 1984. Two bombs did considerable damage to the cab and control equipment, and also to the track. Fortunately the 15.10 Liner train from Adelaide, which was passing on the up line, was not impeded. The line was closed for seventy-two hours, and the large numbers of cross-border Christmas shoppers required up to eleven replacement buses to cover just one service train! No 145 was rebuilt at Inchicore, returning to service in late 1987. It was finally scrapped at Inchicore in August 2006.

No 173 approaches Arklow with the 09.35 Dublin Connolly–Rosslare Harbour on Thursday 12 November 1987. Normal motive power for this train was two Class 121 locomotives but the light load of five Mark 2 coaches was well within the capacity of a single Class 141.

The rail-connected fertiliser factory at Shelton Abbey can be seen in the background. It opened in 1965 and No 071 worked the last bagged fertiliser train from the factory in October 2002. Trainloads of Anhydrous Ammonia arrived here from Marino Point near Cork and the finished bagged fertiliser product was distributed by rail throughout Ireland.

An interesting line-up of locomotives at the south end of Dundalk on Sunday 15 May 1988. Ex GNR(I) V Class V 4-4-0 No 85 Merlin was taking water on its way to Dublin Connolly from Whitehead via Antrim with a single coach, to take over Shannon Railtour on its return journey from Galway. Nos 159 and 172 are stabled beside the driver's rooms, awaiting trains on Monday morning.

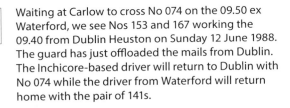

Waiting at Carlow to cross No 074 on the 09.50 ex Waterford, we see Nos 153 and 167 working the 09.40 from Dublin Heuston on Sunday 12 June 1988. The guard has just offloaded the mails from Dublin. The Inchicore-based driver will return to Dublin with No 074 while the driver from Waterford will return home with the pair of 141s.

The guard goes looking for the solitary alighting passenger at Foxford while the lady crossing keeper closes the gates behind No 192 and the two coaches (an ex-BR Mark 1 now in service as a steam heating van and a solitary Park Royal coach – by then at least thirty-four years old) that form the 11.42 Manulla Junction–Ballina on Friday 10 February 1989. This locomotive would spend the day on the branch shuttle, running empty between Manulla Junction and Claremorris each time in order to run round before returning to the isolated Manulla Junction to await connections from the Dublin direction. Foxford station had closed as part of the 1963 rationalisation programme, despite vigorous protests that included physical blocking of the line. Re-opening took place on Monday 7 November 1988, mainly to serve the heavy weekend traffic from the surrounding area to and from Dublin.

The scenic Quagmire Viaduct in deepest Co Kerry as No 181 coasts down the 1 in 100/1 in 162 gradient from Rathmore towards the former Headford Junction with the 15.15 Cork-Tralee on Tuesday 20 June 1989. This locomotive would later work the 18.25 Liner-Mail to Mallow, collecting mails from Tralee, Farranfore and Killarney. The mails were then taken to the sorting office on the down platform at Mallow where they were further sorted for the Travelling Post Office on the 21.30 Cork–Dublin Connolly Liner-Mail service, which waited there from 22.02 to 22.24.

Rosslare Strand on Friday 23 June 1989 where the 17.00 from Waterford has arrived on the right, with No 146 in charge, complete with its battery tail-lamps on the 'Dutch van'. Ten of these bogie brake generating vans to supply electricity and steam heating were designed by Dutch company Werkspoor and built by Dundalk Engineering Works Ltd in 1969. To the left, No 174 prepares to leave with the 18.00 Rosslare Harbour–Dublin Connolly. The normal motive power for this train was two Class 121s and the sectional running was considered 'super express' – a classification that according to the working timetable was "Mark 2 air-conditioned stock only, vacuum brake, maximum speed 75 mph." The service actually took two hours fifty-five minutes for the 105 miles to Dublin Connolly at an average of 36 mph over a route limited to a maximum line speed of 60 mph, plus twenty-four other speed restrictions varying between 5 and 50 mph! The 'super express' classification seems rather optimistic, and No 174 and its lighter train of Mark 2 coaches would have no difficulty in keeping time.

A grey misty day at Coleraine as Nos 152 and 183 arrive with empty Mark 2 carriages for servicing and refuelling on Sunday 11 February 1990. This set had formed the 07.30 GAA Special from Limerick to Ballymoney, arriving there at 13.15. Return was at 17.30, arriving into Limerick at 23.20, making it a long day for the supporters. These carriages for the Special had left Dublin Heuston that morning, forming a 04.00 Special to Limerick.

No 144 approaches the platform ends at Dublin Pearse with the empty carriages from nearby Boston Yard to form the 17.13 to Dundalk on Wednesday 28 March 1990.

No 153 and a short set of Cravens carriages stand in the former boat train platform on the left, forming the 17.25 Dublin Connolly–Arklow. This service was unusually starting from Pearse because of extra DART trains returning from a soccer match between Ireland and Wales at nearby Lansdowne Road. A waiting DART set can just be glimpsed waiting in the distance on the running line behind No 144's train.

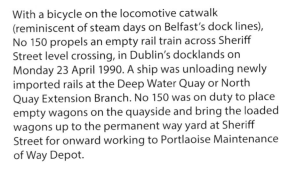

With a bicycle on the locomotive catwalk (reminiscent of steam days on Belfast's dock lines), No 150 propels an empty rail train across Sheriff Street level crossing, in Dublin's docklands on Monday 23 April 1990. A ship was unloading newly imported rails at the Deep Water Quay or North Quay Extension Branch. No 150 was on duty to place empty wagons on the quayside and bring the loaded wagons up to the permanent way yard at Sheriff Street for onward working to Portlaoise Maintenance of Way Depot.

No 150 runs round its three Park Royal coaches and an ex-British Railways van at Cobh on Sunday 10 June 1990, having just arrived with the 14.50 ex Cork. With just 11 minutes allowed for the shunt, No 150 departed for Cork at 15.25. In early 1992 there was a proposal to base a steam preservation society in the former carriage shed, which can be seen on the left. The *Irish Times* published an 'artist's impression' depicting two locomotives with American-style cow-catchers sitting outside the brick shed!

The last few passengers scramble on board the Mark 2 set as ex-works Nos 167 and 158 prepare to leave Sligo with the 17.40 to Dublin Connolly on Friday 28 June 1991.

On the right, the former Dock siding for the end-loading of wheeled vehicles has been disconnected, or 'rationalised', as it would be termed in the weekly circular.

Plenty of time for farewells at Cahir as No 186 waits with the 16.02 Limerick–Rosslare Harbour on Monday 29 June 1992. The timetable was based on maximum 60 mph running after Limerick Junction and with a light train of three Park Royals coaches and a 'Dutch van', there would be no difficulty with the schedule. Indeed, we had to 'wait time' at most stations. The base of the former signal cabin (closed April 1988) is on the right.

No 150 yet again! On this occasion the locomotive is approaching Abbey Junction while returning to Waterford with the 15.15 from Rosslare Harbour on Tuesday 30 June 1992. This extra train (summer weekdays only) ran at 12.45 from Waterford to the Harbour, returning at 15.15. It then formed the regular 17.00 Waterford–Rosslare and return. This extra was poorly supported but at least provided

a chance to sample the South Wexford line in sunshine!

Also in the picture is No 173 with the returning weed-spray train from New Ross. Beside this locomotive there are two diesel fuel tankers to supply the nearby Bus Éireann depot, standing in the heavily overgrown 'garage siding'.

Little Island has an excellent floral display as No 171 stops with the 09.35 Passenger-Mail from Cobh on Wednesday 8 July 1992. Signalmen at this station always kept the standards very high. I often wondered how they managed to find the time as they were kept fairly busy with trains and the manually-operated level crossing gates. The road works for the bypass to Midleton have just started and can be seen above the locomotive.

No 187 has run round and shunted the train to the platform, ready to form the 18.15 Ballina–Manulla Junction on Thursday 24 June 1993. This engine would later run on to Claremorris, run round and return to Manulla to connect with the 18.05 from Dublin Heuston, forming the 21.22 to Ballina. It did not finish there as it would then work the 22.20 Liner train to Dublin North Wall, arriving at 06.40.

Cobh Junction signal cabin is switched in as No 163 working wrong road brings in the 13.45 from Cobh, during single line working on Wednesday 17 August 1994. The permanent way department had occupation of the other line all week while laying new sleepers in the section between Carrigaloe and Rushbrooke.

Variety at Enniscorthy on Thursday 18 August 1994 as No 147 arrives with the 13.35 Dublin Connolly–Rosslare Harbour and No 145 waits in the loop with the 12.50 Balleece–Killinick stone train.

The large boulder stone traffic was loaded over the boundary fence at Balleece, at mile-post 38 in the Rathdrum–Avoca section onto former barytes wagons and unloaded at Killinick for onward transport by road for use in nearby coastal defence works. Former twenty ton magnesite wagons can be seen stored on the extreme right; they were used on the Dolomite traffic from Bennett's Bridge Siding to the Quigley Magnesite factory at Ballinacourty, and then on to a plant at Tivoli near Cork. This lucrative traffic ceased suddenly at the end of April 1982 with the closure of the Ballinacourty plant.

No 171 charges the 1 in 120/1 in 100 gradients on the two and a half mile climb out of Killarney towards Tralee while working the 12.30 from Cork on Sunday 21 August 1994. The permanent way gang are packing up their vans in the foreground while No 121, unusually on its own, waits for signals to return to Mallow after bringing a train of rails to Killarney yard.

The Rose of Tralee Festival was held in Tralee that weekend and Sunday specials to Dublin were at 13.30 (hauled by No 085), and 16.30 (No 147), keeping the Kerry line busy.

Not long out of Inchicore Works, No 158 shunts its train on to the middle road at Drogheda on Saturday 27 May 1995 to clear the down platform for an approaching Modern Railway Society of Ireland railtour from Belfast Yorkgate to Navan and Gorey. To reach Navan, the train was reversed at Mosney, south of Drogheda as being the only safe means of reaching the freight only branch which trails in from the north-west on the downside.

No 150 for the last time (I promise!). On this occasion it was calling at Ashtown, near the Phoenix Park in Dublin while working the 17.15 Dublin Connolly–Longford on Tuesday 2 July 1996. This locomotive would return to Dublin North Wall the same day at 20.20 with a Liner train. Next morning, the engine off the 02.25 Liner Dublin North Wall–Longford would bring this carriage set back to the capital as the 06.15 to Dublin Connolly.

No 150 was named *Inchicore Works 1846–1996*, in both Irish and English at a special ceremony on 15 June 1996 to commemorate the 150th anniversary of Inchicore Works; two of the plates can be seen on the cab sides. Sadly, three had been stolen by persons unknown by early 1998. The last was removed officially for safekeeping.

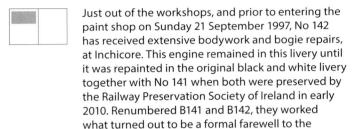

Just out of the workshops, and prior to entering the paint shop on Sunday 21 September 1997, No 142 has received extensive bodywork and bogie repairs, at Inchicore. This engine remained in this livery until it was repainted in the original black and white livery together with No 141 when both were preserved by the Railway Preservation Society of Ireland in early 2010. Renumbered B141 and B142, they worked what turned out to be a formal farewell to the 141's, a Diesel Do rail tour to Longford on a snowy 21 February 2010.

Fresh from the paint shop and receiving mechanical attention, No 162 is at Inchicore on Saturday 23 September 2000. This locomotive was destined to be one of the six serviceable engines at the end of the Class 141 story in February 2010. The final use of a Class 141/181 locomotive in Iarnrod Éireann service was No 171 as Inchicore Works pilot in October 2011, the type having given almost fifty years of useful service.

071 Class

In 1975, the CIÉ Board initiated a programme of modernisation that included higher train speeds and a general improvement in primary routes. This led to the order for eighteen locomotives from General Motors that formed Co-Co Class 071, which had external body styling similar to the preceding Bo-Bo Classes 141/ 181.

The manufacturer's classification was JT 22CW (J = dual cabbed, T = Turbocharged, 22 = model number, C = three axles, W = broad gauge). Weighing almost 100 tons, they were the largest diesel locomotives yet seen in Ireland, with a significant increase in power. The 645E3B 12-cylinder engine produced 2475 hp, more than that provided by a pair of Class 181 locomotives. Delivered in September 1976 and numbered 071–088, after initial testing they did not enter normal service until late May 1977, the delay being caused by a dispute between CIÉ and the drivers' trade unions over manning of the then new Class 071.

They quickly proved their capacity for acceleration and high speeds but initially suffered from rough riding, which was cured by fitting Yaw Dampers. Frame cracking was experienced in the mid-1980s but this was quickly resolved by Inchicore Works. Their absence while repairs were carried out provided an enjoyable interlude for photographers through the temporary substitution of older, smaller locomotives.

These problems aside, Class 071 fulfilled the objective of improved service standards. Some of my best footplate travels were on 071s with a train of Mark 3s, surely the pinnacle of speed and comfort on Ireland's railways. All remain in service in 2015, in the forefront of daily operations on Iarnrod Éireann. Some are in their new all-over grey livery with improbably long fleet numbers, thanks to an EU ruling that will prevent their being mistaken for Belgian or Greek cousins – should they ever meet! Indeed, the 071s are lasting much better than their younger 201 Class cousins.

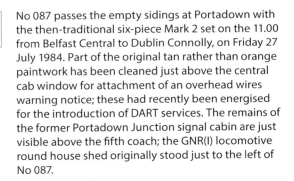

No 087 passes the empty sidings at Portadown with the then-traditional six-piece Mark 2 set on the 11.00 from Belfast Central to Dublin Connolly, on Friday 27 July 1984. Part of the original tan rather than orange paintwork has been cleaned just above the central cab window for attachment of an overhead wires warning notice; these had recently been energised for the introduction of DART services. The remains of the former Portadown Junction signal cabin are just visible above the fifth coach; the GNR(I) locomotive round house shed originally stood just to the left of No 087.

No 076SA gets away past an unusually clear Sallypark yard at Waterford with the 15.25 to Dublin Heuston on Tuesday 8 July 1986. By then, it had received its first re-paint into the more traditional orange, and the CIÉ roundel border on the front of the locomotive is now orange rather than the white

originally applied by GM. The 'S' number suffix indicates that CAWS (Continuous Automatic Warning System) for in-cab signalling has been installed and the 'A' suffix denotes equipment to work air-braked trains. The use of 'SA' was discontinued once all the class had been so fitted.

The white stripe on the body side was a shock at first but it soon blended in, enhancing the appearance when kept clean. Here we can see No 077, not long ex-works at Dublin Heuston, having just arrived with the 07.00 service from Limerick on Monday 4 May 1987.

The blue, white and red paint scheme then being applied to stations seemed inappropriate as it clashed with orange rolling stock. The use of this livery on bare brickwork at, for example, Dublin Connolly was particularly unforgivable.

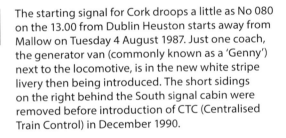

The starting signal for Cork droops a little as No 080 on the 13.00 from Dublin Heuston starts away from Mallow on Tuesday 4 August 1987. Just one coach, the generator van (commonly known as a 'Genny') next to the locomotive, is in the new white stripe livery then being introduced. The short sidings on the right behind the South signal cabin were removed before introduction of CTC (Centralised Train Control) in December 1990.

No 077 again, drawing up at Rathluirc with the 10.40 from Dublin Heuston on Wednesday 15 June 1988. Compare the paintwork with that in the photograph on page 55. The passengers on the low up platform are awaiting the delayed 11.35 from Cork, with a good view of the recently relaid track! CTC reached Charleville, as railwaymen always knew this station, in May 1988, and was extended to Mallow the following December. The signal cabin here was closed in May 1989.

No 082 waits to plunge into an exhaust fume filled tunnel at Cork with the 01.55 Michael Jackson Special to Dublin Heuston on Monday 1 August 1988. This nine-piece Mark 3 train was timetabled to run as required, and is departing early because there were so many returning concert-goers. No 082 had previously arrived with a special from Clonmel. The carriage set from that working returned as the 01.05 to Galway hauled by No 087.

No 082 was named *Institute of Engineers of Ireland* at a ceremony at Dublin Heuston on 11 February 1997, the only class member to carry a name.

Sunday 2 July 1989 was Derby day at the Curragh and No 076 is arriving with racegoers on the 09.15 service from Cork. This train was deferred to a 09.25 departure. No 076's train was grossly overloaded from Limerick Junction onwards with 618 passengers squeezing into accommodation for 496! The preceding 09.15 am special ran non-stop Cork–Curragh, using the set from the 16.45 (Fridays Only) Heuston–Cork. That set returned from the Curragh to Cork at 18.05 and formed the following morning's 05.20 departure for Heuston.

This particular day was also busy at the Cork end. The Gaelic Athletic Association Munster Hurling Finals were being played there, requiring special services from Castleconnell, Thurles, Templemore, Ennis, Dublin and Waterford, bringing a total of 2774 supporters to the City – and then home again!

A rather bedraggled No 077 at Portadown on Thursday 6 September 1990. This was the first day of the two-week closure of the section between there and Lurgan to allow for replacement of the River Bann Bridge, just north of Portadown station.

The NIR set on the right was headed by locomotive No 111 *Great Northern* and its set was tailed by Driving/Brake/First Open No 917, formerly No 813. This vehicle was built by BREL at Derby in 1972 to a Mark 2c design, originally to work with the 1970-built Hunslet locomotives. This train is waiting for bus transfer of passengers from Lurgan and will form the onward 17.00 service from Belfast Central to Dublin Connolly. No 077 waited for its bus passengers and left Portadown at 18.44 in the path of the 18.00 Belfast Central–Dublin Connolly.

Westport-based driver Finbarr Masterson brings No 082 into Manulla Junction on the 13.00 from Dublin Heuston to Westport on a showery Friday 3 July 1992. The Ballina branch set, headed by GM Bo-Bo Class 141 No 154, waits on the left, having brought in the empty stock from Claremorris at 15.40. Both trains were timetabled to depart at 16.17.

Class leader No 071 brings a train of Craven stock and an ex-British Railways van (which had been rebuilt from either a Brake Composite Corridor or a Brake Second Corridor) to a stand at Ballybrophy with the 17.45 Dublin Heuston-Limerick on Saturday 4 July 1992. Evening passenger traffic from Heuston to Limerick was substantial. The previous departure from Heuston was the three stop 17.40 Mark 3 set to Limerick, which ran via the 'direct curve', taking two hours five minutes for the 127 mile run. The 17.45 was a more leisurely affair, formed of Cravens coaches, and ran via the junction platforms, waiting there for 26 minutes to run round and take a connection out of the 18.55 or 19.05 (SO) ex-Cork, thus avoiding the need for a return connecting service from Limerick.

The journey from Ballybrophy to Limerick via Nenagh is actually 5½ miles shorter than the "main route" via Limerick Junction. By a combination of all these factors, the Nenagh branch set, just visible beyond the building on the left, comprising Class 141 No 150 and a short train will leave at 19.10, three minutes after No 071's arrival, but will arrive at Limerick at 20.43, seven minutes before No 071!

Yet another busy Sunday evening in Cork, this time for the GAA Munster Hurling Final on 5 July 1992. No 081 is in charge of the 17.55 return GAA Special to Limerick and No 073 will follow up the (Glanmire) Tunnel with the regular 18.20 non-stop Dublin Heuston service. There were five departures from Cork in just forty-five minutes up to 18.30, one special to Dublin Heuston, another to the Junction, two for Limerick City, and the regular train. The last special train of the day departed at 19.50 on a two hour forty minute non-stop schedule to Heuston, using the Executive Mark 3 set. A total of 2260 supporters travelled on the four specials plus the regular service at 18.20.

The driver of No 080 glances towards Limerick as he rattles over the flat crossing at Limerick Junction with the 07.30 Dublin Heuston–Cork on Wednesday 23 June 1993. In the distance No 084 waits at signals with a 07.30 educational tours special from Waterford to Tralee.

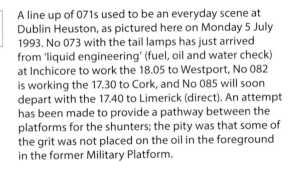

A line up of 071s used to be an everyday scene at Dublin Heuston, as pictured here on Monday 5 July 1993. No 073 with the tail lamps has just arrived from 'liquid engineering' (fuel, oil and water check) at Inchicore to work the 18.05 to Westport, No 082 is working the 17.30 to Cork, and No 085 will soon depart with the 17.40 to Limerick (direct). An attempt has been made to provide a pathway between the platforms for the shunters; the pity was that some of the grit was not placed on the oil in the foreground in the former Military Platform.

No 084 has paused at Athy on the 11.35 Dublin Heuston–Waterford and is waiting to cross No 071 working the 10.50 from Waterford on Tuesday 6 July 1993. On the left, the Inchicore driver of No 084, returning to Dublin, is chatting with the crew of that morning's empty cement train from Limerick to the Tegral siding. This train, headed by Bo-Bo No 167, is just out of sight on the left and waiting to follow No 071 as far as Kildare, before running round and returning to Limerick.

Athy was then a fringe signal box to the main CTC system. The up platform starting signal was a semaphore, but the advance starting signal was electric. Both are visible in the distance.

It was rather like doing lottery numbers to get locomotives posed together in number sequence. Here was my quick-pick selection at Dublin Heuston on the morning of Tuesday 6 July 1993. All three locomotives have been 'hooked off' by the shunter and moved slightly forward on arrival, No 074 on the 07.30 from Tralee, No 072 on the 08.00 from Galway and No 073 on the 07.25 from Westport.

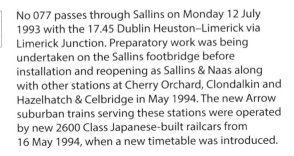

No 077 passes through Sallins on Monday 12 July 1993 with the 17.45 Dublin Heuston–Limerick via Limerick Junction. Preparatory work was being undertaken on the Sallins footbridge before installation and reopening as Sallins & Naas along with other stations at Cherry Orchard, Clondalkin and Hazelhatch & Celbridge in May 1994. The new Arrow suburban trains serving these stations were operated by new 2600 Class Japanese-built railcars from 16 May 1994, when a new timetable was introduced.

On temporary loan to Northern Ireland Railways, No 077 eases the 15.00 Belfast Central–Dublin Connolly through Central Junction and under the Donegall Road Bridge on Tuesday 20 June 1995. The magnetic aerial for the NIR train radio connection with the Control Office at Belfast Central can be seen on the passenger side roof of No 077's cab.

The NIR engineers on the left are working on the crossover, in preparation for the opening of the new station at Great Victoria Street. It was regular practice that Irish Rail would lend Class 071 locomotives to NIR, to cover for repairs etc to Nos 111–113, or when they were on extended use on permanent way duties.

No 088 was the last of the class to receive its engine upgrade from 12-645E3B to 12-645E3C (officially change of turbo and modernised engine management facilities). Having also received extensive bodywork repairs and now ready for the paint shops, it was pictured at Inchicore Works on Wednesday 12 July 1995. The planned re-paint did not materialise, and No 088 returned to traffic in this condition. It was eventually repainted in September 1995.

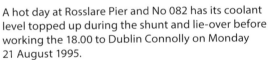

A hot day at Rosslare Pier and No 082 has its coolant level topped up during the shunt and lie-over before working the 18.00 to Dublin Connolly on Monday 21 August 1995.

The chalked notice on the cabside had been applied at Dublin Connolly. It read "Wexford, Rosslare Hbr", and was meant for guidance of passengers at Connolly boarding the 13.38 departure from there at Platform 5, rather than the 13.25 to Sligo from Platform 4.

The 071's received bodywork repairs as required, especially around the cab windows to combat corrosion. Here we can see structural detail of No 075 in the ramps shop at Inchicore on Friday 22 May 1998. This locomotive was in for repairs following an accident on NIR at Finaghy while working the 04.45 cement train from Dundalk to Adelaide Yard on Tuesday 7 April 1988.

It is not what it looks at first glance! No 080 is stabled at Drogheda, next to No 086 which is also stabled, at the head of a train of Tara Mines wagons on Saturday 18 July 1998. The 071s were equipped for multiple working with other class members, CIÉ Classes 121/141/181 and NIR Class 111. However, this feature was seldom used due to weight concerns. The hill to the right in this view was later removed to make room for the new railcar-servicing depot.

201 Class

Increased passenger numbers and the need for faster journey times over premier routes with Mark 3 coaching stock led to the initial order for ten more powerful locomotives in November 1992. General Motors were again the preferred suppliers, this being their fifth order for new locomotives. The manufacturers' designation was JT42HCW (J = export, T = turbocharged, 42 = model number, H = head end power, C = three axle bogies, W = broad gauge). The order was later increased to a total of thirty-four of which two were bought by Northern Ireland Railways to cover their share of motive power obligations on cross-border Enterprise services.

These dual-cabbed locos quickly demonstrated the greater haulage and acceleration characteristics of their 3200 hp type 12-710G3B engines, and their use was soon expanded to freight duties. This hastened the demise of the remaining members of first generation Co-Co Class 001 and allowed GM Class 071 to be cascaded to other services, thus improving reliability all round.

The 201s were to prove an expensive investment, with several enjoying significantly shorter active working lives than earlier diesel types. At acquisition, the utilitarian and ubiquitous modern diesel multiple unit was on the horizon. Further, a downturn in the economy from around 2007 and withdrawal of the Mark 3 coaching stock, led to around 13 of the 34 locomotives being stored at Inchicore at time of writing. Twenty-four of the class had been push-pull equipped on construction, and with their wider sphere of operations, they were favoured for retention in service. In early 2015, remaining passenger duties were confined to Dublin–Cork Mark 4 sets and Dublin–Belfast Enterprise De Dietrich sets, both being push-pull formations. The few remaining Liner trains, mainly from Ballina to Dublin North Wall, are shared by Classes 201 and 071 locomotives.

Class leader No 201 is seen in the Inchicore running shed having just returned with a trial train of Mark 3 coaching stock on Tuesday 12 July 1994. On completion, this locomotive was air-freighted from the General Motors Works near London, Ontario to Dublin via Iceland. The official reason for this expensive mode of shipment was to facilitate driver training and clearance before the arrival of the rest of the class – Nos 202/203 arrived by sea on Thursday 21 July 1994.

No 201 was transported to Inchicore from Dublin Airport on the night of Friday/Saturday 10/11 June 1994. After fitting Radio and CAWS equipment, the first trial run was to Kildare the following Tuesday. This locomotive was stored at Inchicore in late December 2008 after little more than fourteen years' service.

To the left is No 071, class leader of the preceding class to be purchased from General Motors.

On Friday 24 March 1995, Class 181 No 187 hauls brand new No 231 from the delivery ship *Stellanova* and negotiates the roundabout at the Deep Water Quay beside the former Great Southern & Western Railway Point Depot in Dublin. Meanwhile, at the top left of the picture, the next locomotive (No 229) has been unloaded and awaits removal of its protective blue cover. This was the final batch (comprising thirteen locomotives) to arrive at Dublin Docks.

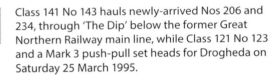

Class 141 No 143 hauls newly-arrived Nos 206 and 234, through 'The Dip' below the former Great Northern Railway main line, while Class 121 No 123 and a Mark 3 push-pull set heads for Drogheda on Saturday 25 March 1995.

Introduced to traffic on Wednesday 8 March 1995, and still quite clean on Saturday 22 April 1995, No 218 races up the final 1 in 198/1 in 390 gradient to Kellystown Summit at milepost 37.25 with an eight-piece Mark 2 set on the 11.00 Belfast Central–Dublin Connolly. Irish Rail had introduced Class 201 to all their cross-border passenger rosters two days earlier. This locomotive was named *River Garavogue* in October 1995.

Just out of the box. Delivered on Friday 24 March 1995 and in service for just four days on Tuesday 25 April 1995, No 228 is pictured from Tates Avenue Bridge in suburban Belfast. The magnetic NIR train radio aerial can just be seen on the cab roof. This locomotive was named *An Abhainn Bhui* in October 1995 (the English equivalent "River Owenea" nameplates have yet to be fitted).

No 228 is being 'notched up', the tail of its train having cleared the curve at Central Junction while working the 18.00 Belfast Central–Dublin Connolly. Permanent Way work was in hand to install pointwork to allow access to Great Victoria Street Station, due to re-open on 30 September 1995.

No 224 accelerates away from a permanent way speed restriction at Lisburn while working the 18.00 Belfast Central–Dublin Connolly on Thursday 27 April 1995. This locomotive was named *Abhainn an Feile/ River Feale* in July 1995.

The one-and-half mile long third line on the left was opened between Lisburn and the former Knockmore Junction on Monday 30 May 1977. Through services to Londonderry (Waterside) were diverted from Belfast York Road to Belfast Central on Monday 23 January 1978, using the former GNR(I) branch between Knockmore Junction and Antrim. The opening of the Dargan Bridge across the River Lagan in Belfast in November 1994, saw these services return to the more traditional NCC route in June 2001 after an upgrade of the Bleach Green Junction to Antrim section.

The new pointwork at Central Junction is almost complete as No 204 *River Barrow* brings the 18.00 Belfast Central–Dublin Connolly under the Donegall Road Bridge on Monday 15 May 1995. At time of writing, No 204 is stored at Inchicore Works.

No 217 *River Flesk* brings a rake of six Cravens coaches and an ex-BR van forming the 15.10 from Westport off the Athlone branch and round the curve into Portarlington on Sunday 2 July 1995. The working timetable noted that rostered motive power was two Class 141s subject to a maximum speed of 100 mph between Portarlington and Dublin. It would be interesting to travel on a Class 141 at this speed, but save the thought as the Cravens carriages were restricted to 75 mph anyway!

It's 'all blue' as unnamed No 209 driven by Belfast-based Gerry Gilmore passes the former signal box at Rush & Lusk on Wednesday 12 July 1995 with the 11.00 Dublin Connolly–Belfast Central. This splendidly turned out nine-coach train in the Inter City sector livery is topped and tailed by generator vans. The third coach is dining car No 547, now preserved and operated by the RPSI.

NIR-owned locomotive No 209 was due to be named *River Foyle* but the nameplates were never fitted.

A busy, smoky scene at Dublin Connolly on Sunday 31 March 1996. On the left, the driver of No 203 *River Corrib* awaits the guard's right-away to start the 15.00 to Belfast Central.

In the centre, Class 121 Nos 130 and 135 stand at Platform 3, ready for the 18.15 Dublin–Sligo, having arrived earlier in the day with the 08.55 from Sligo.

On the right, No 209 waits at Platform 4 with the 18.20 to Belfast Central. The second vehicle of this train is No 904, an ex-British Railways Mark 2F First Open coach, (previously BR No 3367) which was purchased by NIR in 1988 to cater for increased first class, cross-border traffic. The third vehicle is grill/bar/dining car No 546 (formerly BR No M1800), which was purchased by NIR in 1982.

Catering staff referred to No 546 as the 'Electric Car' and to No 547 as the 'Gas Car', based on differing types of kitchen cooker in each vehicle.

No 208 *River Lagan* gets underway with the 10.00 Belfast Central–Dublin through Adelaide Halt on Sunday 30 March 1997. This Sunday service was usually heavier than the corresponding weekday train, to cater for traditional returning weekend traffic from Dublin.

Two NIR sets left Connolly less than half an hour apart on the Sunday evening. The 17.55 departure ran non-stop to Newry, while the 18.20 made the more traditional stops, including Mosney in the summer months and Botanic for the students at nearby Queen's University, Belfast. The third line on the left ran from Adelaide freight yard (behind the photographer) to the nearby Guinness depot, and was also used for Smithwicks and Harp keg traffic. Wagons for the Guinness yard were hauled from Adelaide to a headshunt and then propelled into the siding, usually by an Irish Rail locomotive.

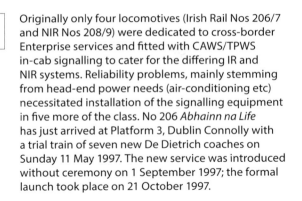

Originally only four locomotives (Irish Rail Nos 206/7 and NIR Nos 208/9) were dedicated to cross-border Enterprise services and fitted with CAWS/TPWS in-cab signalling to cater for the differing IR and NIR systems. Reliability problems, mainly stemming from head-end power needs (air-conditioning etc) necessitated installation of the signalling equipment in five more of the class. No 206 *Abhainn na Life* has just arrived at Platform 3, Dublin Connolly with a trial train of seven new De Dietrich coaches on Sunday 11 May 1997. The new service was introduced without ceremony on 1 September 1997; the formal launch took place on 21 October 1997.

A three-piece De Dietrich set heads south at Gormanston on Wednesday 20 May 1998, comprising an All First, Diner, and Driving Brake First Open No 9004. This train had started at Dundalk and was running as a relief to the 16.10 from Belfast Central. The short set had departed Dublin Connolly at 15.30 as empty stock, arriving Dundalk at 16.21. Departure from Dundalk was at 17.15, (eleven minutes in front of the 16.10 from Belfast), calling at Drogheda, and arriving Connolly at 18.10, 10 minutes ahead of the heavily loaded normal scheduled service.

The spare De Dietrich set was often used on relief trains around this time – especially the 06.50 Dundalk–Dublin on Saturdays, and the Dublin Connolly–Dundalk Sunday service. The set also covered Dublin outer suburban links when no other stock was available.

Gormanston signal cabin was closed on Sunday 4 February 1990. The upper floor is now preserved at Dromod on the restored section of the Cavan & Leitrim Railway, moving there by road on 15 August 1999.

CIÉ, Irish Rail and Iarnrod Éireann Railcars
(Diesel and Electric)

My observations of CIÉ railcars (usually referred to as multiple units in the UK) started with the last of the 1950s-vintage diesel-powered AECs, through the 1984 introduction of the overhead electric fleet of Dublin Area Rapid Transit (DART) and on to the seemingly endless tsunami of modern railcars from 1994 forward. These recent arrivals, including some types that were significantly more useful than others, marked the decline of locomotive haulage throughout the island of Ireland. I have always found the traditional locomotive and train formation more appealing, and this change in the face of the railway helped the decision to give up lineside photography, and to concentrate my hobby indoors in the form of historical research and writing.

The last duties of the old AEC railcars were on the Bray–Greystones shuttle, and the Dublin Connolly–Maynooth service. Unit No 6107 seen here is about to start with the 21.57 Bray–Greystones on Tuesday 21 August 1984. It was quite a shock to leave the warm, modern, brightly-lit interior of a then brand new DART set, and board this creaking, musty, cold and intermittently illuminated relic for its trundle around Bray Head to Greystones.

No 6107 was built in late 1953 as a Driving Motor Brake Composite No 2640 seating twelve first class and thirty-two tourist class passengers, and was converted to all standard class around 1971. The engines were removed in 1973 on conversion to push-pull driving trailer. It was withdrawn in September 1987, and scrapped at Dundalk in July 1989. Sister car No 6111 (originally No 2624) lingered on at Inchicore in decrepit condition having been withdrawn the same day as No 6107, until its transfer for preservation at Downpatrick in February 2015.

The driving controls of No 6107, as seen on Friday 5 April 1985 working the 14.47 push-pull from Bray to Greystones, while the driver was out on the ground

attending to yet another fault! The cab looks rather nautical with greenhouse style heaters below the large picture windows. The main power control is the dual lever affair in the middle, one for forward and the other for reverse. The train brake control handle is in the foreground beside the red, wheel-operated handbrake. 'Footplate Pass' passengers on this railcar did not have the luxury of a seat, and a milk crate had to suffice.

The loaded tanker cars for that evening's Sligo Esso Liner train are worked along the Alexander tramway on Monday 14 February 1994 by a Dublin Port tractor, as newly-delivered (Arrow type) Class 2600 railcar No 2604 is prepared for placing on its bogies on a piece of straight track. The obligatory red flag to warn of danger is being carried by the train guard on the right who didn't even wear a clean coat for this special occasion. No 2604 entered traffic on Monday 16 May 1994 along with most of the rest of the class. In early 2015, the 2600 fleet is based in the Cork area.

Newly delivered No 2701 (with original small digit numerals), basks in the sunshine outside the ramps shop at Inchicore on Friday 22 May 1998. It waited nearly a year before entering service on Monday 19 April 1999. These Spanish-built railcars were nicknamed 'Sparrows', derived from 'Spanish Arrows', as opposed to the Japanese-built Class 2600 which then carried the commuter brand 'Arrow'. Class 2700 were built by GEC-Alsthom and had a short working life as the entire class of twenty-seven vehicles had been stored at Limerick and Inchicore by April 2013.

Three of the four DART sets of Class 8500, newly-delivered from the Toyku Car Corporation of Japan, await commissioning at the cleared Inchicore scrap sidings on Saturday 23 September 2000. They would eventually enter service in May 2001, formed up into four-car sets as pictured. Two more batches of this type were later delivered, Class 8510 comprising four similar sets entered service in 2002. Then ten sets of Class 8520 with a slightly different appearance arrived in 2004/5.

On the extreme left can be seen two 30 ft six-wheel coaches, Nos 478A/53M and 479A/39M of 1890s vintage that had been recovered from the closed Great Southern Railway Preservation Society depot at Mallow. They are covered with the blue tarpaulins that had once protected Class 201 for their voyage across the Atlantic on delivery from General Motors.

An impressive line up of Class 2900 railcars, headed up by No 2912, in the stabling sidings at Dundalk on Saturday 4 October 2003. Commissioning of this class comprising twenty-nine four-car sets, built by CAF Spain in two batches, was carried out expeditiously. Originally intended to be numbered 29001–29029, these vehicles are known by their individual unit numbers. The set numbers are used principally for rostering purposes.

The first of the third class of Japanese-built DART vehicles awaits its pre-delivery inspection at the former Dun Laoghaire boat train platform at Pearse Station, Dublin on Saturday 1 May 2004. Class 8520 as they were to be known, have slightly different front end styling compared to their Class 8500 and 8510 sisters. Co-incidentally, the pre-delivery inspections of the original 1984 DART cars was carried out at the same platform! These latest units have air conditioning and are close coupled in ten sets of four vehicles, like the other DART vehicles from Japan. The unit depicted, No 8621 was among the first of this class to be delivered (on 23 April 2004), and entered service in January 2005.

Mark 2 Carriages

By the end of the 1960s it was recognised that the youngest passenger vehicles in service (the 1963–1967 built Cravens coaches) failed to meet the quality standards expected of a modern railway. The first of a new generation of vacuum-braked, air-conditioned passenger coaches appeared in 1972, constructed by British Rail Engineering at Derby. The design closely conformed with the Mark 2D type then entering service on British Rail. The principal differences lay in the Irish version being vacuum-braked whereas BR used air brakes. Also, on-train services were powered by twin Detroit generators housed in purpose-designed Generator Vans built by BREL at Litchurch Lane, Derby. These unique vehicles were to Mark 2 body profile and also contained two luggage compartments and guard accommodation. They were gangway-equipped and fitted also with a passenger corridor.

The introduction of this 73-strong fleet was revolutionary and well received by the travelling public. 'Supertrain' Mark 2Ds remained in the forefront of passenger services between Dublin and Cork until the introduction of the Mark 3s in 1984, when they were cascaded onto the Belfast, Sligo and Rosslare routes. Sadly, the manner in which the Mark 2Ds were phased out eroded much of the passenger goodwill that these modern, comfortable coaches had generated. They were replaced by hard-seated new railcar stock, and poor rostering resulted in chronic overcrowding on many services.

There was genuine regret among enthusiasts, and more importantly the travelling public, to see these fine coaches withdrawn. The final working of a Mark 2D set was on Monday 31 March 2008 and scrapping of some of these vehicles commenced the next day, such was the hurry to get them out of service.

Despite the burgeoning penchant for railcars, they could not be delivered fast enough to meet growing demand. As an interim measure, sixteen second-hand Mark 2Cs were purchased from BR in late 1990. These coaches were air-braked, fully refurbished at Inchicore for Irish service and marshalled into two sets of eight. They were replaced in 2003 by the railcars that were *officially* regarded as superior – passengers had a rather different opinion.

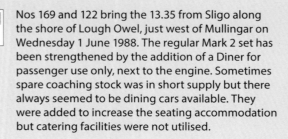

Nos 169 and 122 bring the 13.35 from Sligo along the shore of Lough Owel, just west of Mullingar on Wednesday 1 June 1988. The regular Mark 2 set has been strengthened by the addition of a Diner for passenger use only, next to the engine. Sometimes spare coaching stock was in short supply but there always seemed to be dining cars available. They were added to increase the seating accommodation but catering facilities were not utilised.

No 079 heads the 18.00 Belfast Central–Dublin Connolly past Adelaide Halt, Belfast on Sunday 22 April 1990. The two coaches next to the engine are former first class vehicles (number series 5101–5106) and are recognisable by the seven windows in the body side compared to eight for standard class. When new, they accommodated forty-two first class passengers in a pleasant two plus one across seating arrangement. Later five of the six carriages were downgraded to standard class with seating for fifty-six or sixty-two passengers. No 5106 is now operated by the RPSI and numbered 304 in their fleet.

Delivered the previous day, ex-BR Mark 2C is at Inchicore on Friday 25 May 1990 undergoing ultrasonic inspection. This coach was built in December 1970 as a forty-two seat first open (BR No 3156), and was re-classified as BR second class in 1983 (becoming No 6406). There were eighteen coaches in the single build lot of Mark 2C FOs of which five came to Irish Rail and one to NIR! It was extensively refurbished at Inchicore and became Irish Rail No 4103, entering service on 7 December 1990. It was withdrawn on 4 November 2003 along with the rest of the Mark 2 air-braked fleet when Class 2900 railcars were substituted.

Many thought that the Tippex stripe was painted on! Here No 4104 (formerly BR No 3154/6105) has its stripes applied in the paint shop on Thursday 13 September 1990 before entering service on 1 December 1990. This coach was withdrawn on 4 November 2003 and was returned to the UK for final scrapping, after removal of spares by the RPSI to help keep their own fleet of Mark 2 coaches running.

No 078 brings the 10.50 from Waterford into Carlow on Monday 3 June 1991. The train is formed of a rake of ex BR Mark 2C air-braked stock, including the buffet car (either No 4401 or 4402), fifth from the engine. The kinked siding on the right was once used for discharging oil, and runs behind the down platform to the cement store and small goods yard. The remains of the former cattle bank can be seen on the right with a chain link fence along its edge.

Nos 157 and 146 with a rake of Mk2's cross the Royal Canal at the site of the former lifting bridge at Newcomen Bridge Junction with the 18.30 from Platform 7 at Connolly Station to Sligo on Friday 21 June 1991. In the left background, an unidentified Class 141 locomotive shunts a long train of wagons under West Road Cabin. The under bridge for the Royal Canal was reduced to culvert in the 1960s but a new lifting bridge was installed and opened on Tuesday 15 May 2001 allowing boat traffic once again to enter the Royal Canal from Spencer Dock.

Major changes were scheduled for the following weekend with the implementation of the Connolly West signalling project at North Strand Junction, West Road, Church Road, Glasnevin Junction and Cabra, necessitating temporary train diversions such as this one. The normal route for Sligo services was Dublin Connolly–West Road Junction–North Strand Junction–Glasnevin Junction–Liffey Junction.

Pictured from the footbridge at Ballinasloe, No 084 arrives with the 14.05 from Dublin Heuston on Saturday 22 June 1991. This train crossed the 15.10 up Day Mail from Galway at Ballinasloe, which was being worked by No 072.

The train of Mk2 air-braked stock is led by one of the 1969 Dundalk-built Werkspoor 'Dutch vans', three of which were converted to provide power for ventilation and lighting to the train set. Two of these vans have been preserved by the RPSI, Nos 3158 and 3163/4602. They are now numbered as RPSI 462 and 625.

Irish Rail Mark 2 air-braked sets rarely worked cross-border. However, here is a view of Platform 1 at Belfast Central on Sunday 8 March 1992 with No 083 and a Mark 2C set. This train had worked from Tullamore to Belfast on a 07.35 Birr GAA Special, arriving at 11.20. Return from Belfast was at 18.20, the journey taking just over four hours including Customs inspection at Dundalk and reversal at Dublin Connolly.

Mk2c No 4105, formerly BR first open No 3163/6401, entered Irish traffic on Thursday 19 December 1991, and was broken up by a contractor at Inchicore on Saturday 21 February 2004.

A bright summer's evening at Rosslare Strand, as No 146 single-handedly works the 18.00 Rosslare Harbour–Dublin Connolly on Thursday 1 July 1993. The train has pulled well up to allow the guard's van at the rear of the train to reach the platform. The crossing train on the right is the 17.00 Waterford–Rosslare, later to form the 19.40 from there to Limerick.

The Mark 2 set has been strengthened by the addition of a dining car next to the engine. No 146 is now preserved in working order by the Irish Traction Group and can be seen operating trains at Downpatrick.

No 080 brings an eight-piece Mark 2D rake across Glasnevin Junction with the 07.45 from Sligo on Friday 19 November 1993. Most of the locomotive rosters on the Sligo line had been taken over by the Class 071 the previous month, with a resultant improvement in timekeeping. Permanent Way men on the right of No 080 look on as the engine crosses the point-work leading to the line to Islandbridge Junction. New track panels can just be seen in the background above the first coach.

No 212 *River Slaney* is about to dive below the twin-arched Ormeau Road Bridge, past the former gasworks wall as it leaves Belfast Central with the ten Mark 2 coaches forming the 18.00 to Dublin Connolly on Wednesday 21 June 1995. Belfast Central Station is just out of sight beyond the train.

No 073 restarts across Howth Junction with the 10.58 Dundalk–Dublin Connolly (July and August only) on Monday 21 August 1995. This train was allowed ninety-four minutes for its fifty-four mile journey from Dundalk to Dublin, stopping all stations to Howth Junction except Portmarnock. The guard peers out of No 4602's compartment window, enduring the noise, vibration and diesel fumes as he approaches journey's end. No 4602 (formerly 3163) is currently in store at the RPSI depot at Whitehead, Co Antrim.

The Mark 2 vacuum-braked stock remained generally in the same livery as originally applied in 1972, apart from the change of colour from a golden brown to the corporate orange. White stripes were added in the early 1990s, and one set received a special livery for use on the Galway line (see above). One final detail change was application of grey paint to the roofs of some vehicles, as on standard open No 5230 at Dublin Heuston on Tuesday 6 October 1998. The premises of the Irish Railway Record Society are in the background.

No 5230 was delivered in bottle green undercoat to Dublin on 19 September 1972 and, after minor finishing at Inchicore, it entered service on 4 December 1972. It was scrapped at Inchicore on 20 January 2007.

One set of nine Mark 2s was refurbished and received a new livery similar to that used on Class 201 locomotives, entering service as a set as the 17.05 (FO) to Cork on 20 July 2001. The work involved tackling corrosion problems, especially around the toilet areas, new interiors and general updating. The total cost was reportedly one million Euro! The refurbished set worked mainly on Galway to Dublin Heuston links.

In this photograph No 5225 is on stands at Inchicore on Saturday 23 September 2000 receiving attention to under-floor equipment and has yet to receive its black roof.

Mark 3 Carriages

The severe accident at Buttevant in August 1980 led to a long-overdue review of investment in CIÉ. Unfortunately, it took another severe accident at Cherryville in August 1983 effectively to crystallise concerns about the consequences of underinvestment. In October 1981, the Irish government announced a project to acquire new coaching stock. The supply contract went to British Rail Engineering Ltd with the rather optimistic intention that deliveries would commence "late 1983" in what was to prove the only export sale of Mark 3 coaches.

There were several negotiated changes in the size of the contract prior to and during delivery but eventually there were 125 vehicles in the fleet, based on the Mark 3 type that had been developed for use with British Rail's 125 mph High Speed Trains, introduced in 1976. Externally the Mark 3 was similar to the Mark 2D type but technically considerably more advanced, employing monocoque construction with an all-welded mild steel stressed skin of exceptional strength. Most of the UK fleet remains in traffic, and continues to give excellent high-speed services after working lives of around forty years.

The Irish contract was executed in two phases, the first in 1984–86 comprised fifty-six vehicles that were supplied by BREL. Some vehicles were delivered virtually complete, requiring only minor finishing work while the remainder were shipped either as body shells or as kits of parts with assembly/construction at Inchicore.

The remaining sixty-eight vehicles were constructed entirely at Inchicore under licence in 1986–89. At the time, there was an urgent need for more and better suburban stock. It was decided to adapt twenty-four of this batch for use in five push-pull sets. Five coaches were therefore specially modified as Driving Trailers (Nos 6101–5) to work in these configurations.

The first bodyshell had arrived in December 1983, and enough coaches were completed for a press launch in May 1984 with the first two sets entering traffic in July 1984. The Mark 3 stock was probably the best that we were to see in Ireland, very comfortable and smooth running. The 'plug' doors caused some problems that took time to resolve but once that was done, they gave excellent service.

Introduction of the Mark 4 coaches on the Cork line, and the Class 22000 railcars nationwide, sealed the fate of the Mark 3s. The entire fleet, including push-pull vehicles were in store by September 2009. The total fleet size of 124 had been augmented by purchase from BR of ex-HST TRFK No E40513, which was converted by Interfleet Technology in the UK. This vehicle cost £1 million to purchase and convert, becoming café bar car No 6402, entering service on 19 April 2002 and giving only seven years' service in Ireland. At time of writing, 21 Mark 3 vehicles survive: 11 for future service with the Belmond International Cruise Train; three are preserved at the West Clare Railway, Moyasta; three are retained by Iarnrod Éireann for possible use with the new weed-spray train; four are in use as Generator Vans providing head-end power on the Dublin–Belfast Enterprise service.

A further excursion into this type of stock concerned the ten-coach International Set built by British Rail Engineering. Launched in September 1986 and used initially on Euston–Manchester services, some were displayed at Hamburg in May 1988 at a transport exhibition. Sadly no export orders in continental Europe resulted and the entire set of ten was purchased by CIÉ in 1994. They were rewired and refitted at Inchicore in 1995/6 being then reclassified by CIÉ as Mark 3A stock. They were numbered in the 6000 series to denote push-pull capability but conversion of the designated driving trailer (No 6501) was not completed (it became a paint shop trial vehicle and was eventually scrapped). The ex-International Train vehicles were stored in April 2008, some being scrapped together with the Mark 3 fleet. The fate of the remainder is described later in this chapter.

Considering the efficiency of Britain's Mark 3s, still giving good service after much longer working lives, the economics of abandonment of the Irish version appears questionable.

Howth Junction on Monday 12 July 1993, 6101 heads up a six-piece Mark 3 push-pull set powered by an unidentified 121 locomotive while working the 13.00 from Drogheda to Dublin Connolly. 123 on the left, is at the down platform waiting for the right away with another six-piece push-pull set, forming the 13.44 from Dublin Pearse to Drogheda. Twenty four of the batch of 68 Mark 3 vehicles constructed at Inchicore were built as push-pull vehicles. Five coaches (6101–6105) were adapted as 'Driving Brake Generator Second Class', better known as 'Control Cars' with full width cabs and underfloor Cummins generators for on-board train services. Nineteen coaches (6301–6319) were built to run with the control cars and until the arrival of the 201 class the 121's struggled with the heavy trains. The coaches had alternate opening 'hopper' windows which proved useful when the feeble air conditioning broke down.

The requirement for First Class travel, particularly on the Cork line, meant that Standard Class vehicles would sometimes be pressed into service as First Class. Here we see the interior of fairly recently introduced 7114 at Dublin Heuston on Monday 27 January 1986 with the addition of orange curtains and antimacassars. The central aisle carpet is anything but first class; shunters after uncoupling the locomotives of incoming trains would always walk through the train looking for newspapers and magazines, carrying oil and grease the full length of the train. A lesson was learned as the central aisle floor in the later push-pull carriages was covered with more resilient material that was easily cleaned. This superficial dressing of an otherwise standard class coach, and labelling it 'First' was unsuccessful. Eventually the first class business passenger was properly catered for with the introduction of City Gold and Executive brandings.

The old and the new at Ballybrophy, as No 075 arrives with a Mark 3 set on the 08.20 from Limerick on Thursday 17 July 1986. The train on the right is the 08.10 from Limerick via Nenagh, scheduled to arrive one minute before No 075. Time keeping on the branch was easy and No 185 has already run-round its train. The green signal on the down side beyond the signal cabin is for the approaching 08.50 Dublin Heuston–Tralee. Connecting passengers for Limerick via Nenagh will cross the footbridge to No 185's train, due to depart at 10.05.

Generator Van No 7611 nears completion at Inchicore on Saturday 13 September 1986, with one of the two Cummins generators in the foreground ready for lowering into the compartment. A Mark 3 body shell can be glimpsed on the left undergoing structural work prior to fitting out. Four of these generator vans have recently been adapted to work with the De Dietrich push-pull stock on the cross-border Enterprise. No 7611 was less fortunate, being one of a dozen Mark 3s scrapped at Waterford, succumbing to the cutter's torch in April 2014.

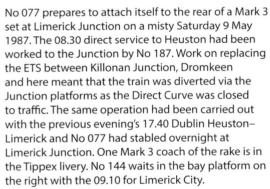

No 077 prepares to attach itself to the rear of a Mark 3 set at Limerick Junction on a misty Saturday 9 May 1987. The 08.30 direct service to Heuston had been worked to the Junction by No 187. Work on replacing the ETS between Killonan Junction, Dromkeen and here meant that the train was diverted via the Junction platforms as the Direct Curve was closed to traffic. The same operation had been carried out with the previous evening's 17.40 Dublin Heuston–Limerick and No 077 had stabled overnight at Limerick Junction. One Mark 3 coach of the rake is in the Tippex livery. No 144 waits in the bay platform on the right with the 09.10 for Limerick City.

This view of No 080 rounding the Direct Curve at Limerick Junction with the 08.30 Limerick–Dublin Heuston on Friday 7 August 1987 was taken through the window of the dining car. This was the premier train of the day from Limerick, allowed two hours ten minutes for the three-stop 127-mile journey.

A conference takes place underneath No 7166 alongside No 7168 in the carriage building shop at Inchicore on Wednesday 19 August 1987. Both carriages were destined to be fitted out as composites, seating sixteen first class and fifty-two standard class. The first class section was particularly useful on Mayo line trains as quite often, if I was not on the engine, I would join the guard and the checker next to their noisy van in relative comfort, and devoid of first class passengers too! After withdrawal of the Mark 3 fleet in 2009, both 7166 and 7168 languished at North Wall, until they were hauled north for cutting up at Adelaide Yard, Belfast, in mid-2014.

A newly assembled Mark 3 coach at Inchicore carriage building shops on Wednesday 19 August 1987. The coach sides can be seen undergoing construction in the jigs on the right. The completed sides were then welded to an underframe. The corrugated roof and coach ends gave a very strong tubular body designed to stay intact in the event of a derailment. When the body shell was finished, it was moved by crane onto stands to allow the fitting of the modular under-floor equipment. Then it was placed on bogies for fitting out the interior.

The finished article. Here is a sparkling No 7140, almost the last of the first batch, ex-works in the Inchicore trials train at Ballybrophy on Thursday 16 June 1988. The trial train comprised locomotive No 188, coach No 7140 and van No 7602, and ran from Inchicore to Ballybrophy stopping at Kildare and Portarlington in both directions to check No 7140 before it entered service. This coach was eventually scrapped at Dublin North Wall in August 2014 having given just under 20 years' service.

Fellow railway enthusiasts Tony Gray and David Hegarty chat with the catering crew of the Executive Train during the lie-over in Cork with the Cantrell & Cochrane charter train for the Michael Jackson concert on Saturday 30/Sunday 31 July 1988. The bar coach, No 7161, was fitted out to work with coach No 7162, both of which had flexible seating arrangements.

The tables are set for the return journey, and a full meal service was provided to passengers in their seats. This set, as Special No 41, with locomotive No 085, returned to Dublin Heuston non-stop at 00.01 on the 31st. At time of writing, No 7161 is in store at Inchicore Works. No 7162 was cut up at Inchicore in September 2013.

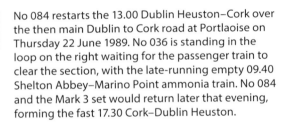

No 084 restarts the 13.00 Dublin Heuston–Cork over the then main Dublin to Cork road at Portlaoise on Thursday 22 June 1989. No 036 is standing in the loop on the right waiting for the passenger train to clear the section, with the late-running empty 09.40 Shelton Abbey–Marino Point ammonia train. No 084 and the Mark 3 set would return later that evening, forming the fast 17.30 Cork–Dublin Heuston.

Fitting out Mark 3 No 7133 to Citygold at Inchicore on Thursday 21 January 1993. Three of the Mark 3 coaches were converted, Nos 7104/7133/7156, each providing a luxurious environment for forty-eight passengers, ably assisted by a Hostess, who provided first class passengers with in-seat meals on the main early, mid-day and tea-time trains from Dublin and Cork. A supplement of IE£15 was charged for a single journey on peak-time trains, IE£3 on Sundays.

Nearly-completed No 7104 at Inchicore on Thursday 21 January 1993 when the panic was on to get the coach ready for its ministerial and press launch a week later!

The electrically operated seating was aligned with the windows, two plus one across the coach, and the tables had a small folding leaf to enable easier access for the more portly businessman. A Pullman style table lamp at the window was above a console which contained Citygold notepaper and a red call button to alert the Hostess to bring a chunky phone/fax machine to plug in to a socket at your table! A very informative panel was provided in each coach detailing all the Irish suppliers who provided the equipment and materials for these superbly fitted-out vehicles.

No 076 waits in the bay platform at Waterford on Saturday 4 September 1993 with a sparkling set of Mark 3s, forming a return working to Dublin conveying invited guests and dignitaries who had earlier that day attended the opening of the new port at Belview. The Special left Heuston at 08.10, running directly to Belview, and returned empty to Waterford for stabling. The pile of peat under the tarpaulin on the right is to keep the signalman in the Central cabin warm in the winter. The steps up to the cabin can just be seen above the first and second coach of No 076's train.

No 081 gets the 17.30 Dublin Heuston–Cork underway and past the recently reopened (16 May 1994) halt at Clondalkin on Wednesday 15 June 1994. The train on the left is the 15.15 from Waterford hauled by No 078 with another Mark 3 set, which was slowed by signals on the approach to Heuston, no doubt caused by the usual wait for an empty platform road.

Recently-delivered ex-BR International Set coach No 99521/Irish Rail No 6201, is inside the carriage building shop at Inchicore on Tuesday 12 July 1994. There would eventually be a single working set of nine of these vehicles, classified as Mk3A by Irish Rail, (not to be confused with the BR Mk3a classification). No 6201 entered traffic on 27 October 1995, and was withdrawn in April 2008 with the rest of her Mk3A sisters, and was cut up at Inchicore in September 2009.

The number series 6201-6208 (suggesting push-pull operation) was allocated to these all-open coaches. No 6401 was the buffet car and the generator vans were from the regular Mk3, 7601–15 number series. One vehicle from the original order (BR No 99520/Irish Rail No 6501) was intended to be a push-pull driving trailer for use with the other 3As, but the conversion was abandoned.

No 085 brings the 09.00 Radio Train Executive Special from Dublin Heuston into Cobh on Thursday 17 August 1995. The two coaches (Nos 7161/7162) at the rear of the train are in the Maroon livery of the then Executive Train brand.

The mobile permanent way gang are undertaking crossover repairs. No 085 will be shortly using this crossover to run round its train and shunt before working the return Special at 18.30.

The crossover at Cobh was infrequently used since the withdrawal of locomotive-hauled stock and the introduction of railcars.

The overall maroon livery on No 7161 is shown off to good effect in this view from an overbridge at Cobh on Thursday 17 August 1995. The two vehicles painted in this attractive livery entered service on a Belfast–Killarney Special working on 9 March 1995, returning to Belfast the following day.

No 078 hauls the empty carriages of the 10.00 Special from Waterford, for the GAA Leinster Hurling Semi-Finals, out of Dublin Connolly towards Pearse on Sunday 22 June 1997. The empty set later returned to Heuston at 12.55 to form the 14.15 to Galway.

The flatter side and deeper window profile of the Mark 3A International Set can be easily seen. By this time the carriages were branded *Cu na Mara* (which means "hound of the sea") and mainly rostered on Dublin Heuston–Galway services.

Mark 3 coach No 7167 was built at Inchicore and introduced to service in 1987 as a composite, seating sixteen first and fifty-two standard class passengers. It was later modified by re-locating the internal partition and re-configuring the seats for thirty-two first class (super-standard) and thirty-six standard class seats. It is pictured with this revised arrangement at Dublin Heuston on Saturday 19 September 1998. The first class section is denoted by a sticker on the plug door and lower down on the windows. A slight livery detail change is the grey roof, which I thought improved their appearance. The addition of the plum thumbnail around the plug door denoted first class, but how many passengers actually understood its purpose? No 7167 was scrapped at Waterford in April 2014 after a period in store.

Mark 3A 6201 is fresh from the paint shop at Inchicore on Sunday 11 September 1994. Compare this photograph with that taken of the same vehicle shortly after arrival at Inchicore twelve weeks earlier on page 103. Some minor flooring repairs are underway at the first class end. With thirty first class seats and twenty-four standard class seats, this vehicle usually ran as standard class. It was withdrawn with the rest of the Mark 3A fleet in April 2008 and cut up at Inchicore in August 2009 together with Nos 6202/6208/6401 and 6501. Coaches Nos 6203/6205 were moved to a hotel in Kildare, and are now derelict. Coaches 6204/6206/6207 were shipped to an RAF depot in Cumbria and destroyed in testing in April 2010, thus ending the International Train Mark 3A story.

NIR 80 Class on loan to CIÉ

Three NIR 80 Class railcar sets were hired by Irish Rail as a temporary measure between 19 October 1987 and 26 November 1990 for suburban work, pending the introduction of the Mark 3 push-pull sets. The railcars were mainly intended for use on Bray–Greystones, Dublin Connolly–Maynooth, and Cork–Cobh services. They were also used on Special train workings and one set even managed to use the triangle at Limerick Junction for turning!

Three power cars were mainly involved (Nos 68/69/86) together with intermediate coaches Nos 761/772/767, and the driving trailers Nos 735/737/740. CAWS (Continuous Automatic Warning System) was fitted to Nos 69 and 737 and for a time to Nos 86 and 735 but removed prior to their return to NIR. General day-to-day maintenance was carried out at Dublin Connolly and Cork running sheds, but the NIR workshops at York Road, Belfast, continued to carry out planned servicing and major repairs.

The combination of Nos 69-772-735 waits to depart from the bay platforms at Dun Laoghaire with the 07.23 on Sunday 31 January 1988. This train was lightly used at first but as its popularity grew, it became a six-piece set. The front portion continued on to Dublin Heuston, arriving at 08.05 while the rear portion worked back from Connolly at 08.01 to Dun Laoghaire as a boat train! Arrival at Heuston early on a Sunday was quite an experience. I expected it to be quiet but queues for the first train of the day, the 08.50 to Tralee, were already forming.

The reopening to Midleton was just a dream at the time as No 68 calls at Cobh Junction (now renamed Glounthaune) while working the 16.50 from Cobh on Wednesday 15 June 1988. The starting signal on the extreme left was for Youghal, the one on the right was for Cobh. The signal cabin here was mostly switched out and the rusty branch rails show no evidence of any recent working.

No 68 approaches the former signal cabin and calls at the staggered platforms at Rushbrooke on the 18.20 from Cobh on Wednesday 15 June 1988. "Mind the gap" would have been a very appropriate announcement at Cobh line stations because, when using the Class 80 sets, there was a considerable climb up to the footboard, never mind a daunting drop down from the train to the platform for the less able.

737-68 departs Cork with the 11.20 to Cobh on Wednesday 15 June 1988. Meanwhile on the left No 123 shunts the TPOs and vans before being turned to work the 15.05 up Day Mail to Dublin Heuston. Several Cork drivers said that this train was their chance to get rid of their worst engine – unfortunately, Inchicore would just as quickly send it back! On the right, No 147 is recovering track panels from yet more 'rationalisation' taking place in the yard in front of the carriage sheds.

The GAA Munster Senior Hurling Championships (Cork vs Clare) at Thurles on Sunday 19 June 1988 required three specials from Cork at 10.00, 10.20 and 10.40, one from Ennis at 10.25, and another from Mallow at 11.35. The six-piece NIR railcars worked a lightly loaded special with ninety-nine passengers at 10.05 from Heuston and here we can see them at the platform, waiting for their return at 17.45. A total of 2157 passengers used the various specials to travel to the match at Thurles.

Incidentally on the same day there was a GAA All-Ireland Hurling Final at Croke Park, Dublin which required three specials from Waterford, Clara and Rosslare, another fairly regular special from Killarney to Dublin Heuston, and a Showtime Special from Galway, again to Heuston. The Sunday (mornings only) Westport to Athlone service was specially extended through to Dublin, with a resultant special train to work its return from Athlone back to Westport. The demand on rolling stock on an already busy Sunday afternoon was high, hence the use of the railcars to Thurles.

A sparkling combination of Nos 737-68 stands at Rathdrum while working the 11.27 Bray–Arklow on Friday 24 June 1988. This enjoyable 37-mile, one hour run arrived in Arklow at 12.28, returning to Bray at 12.35, so not much time for a station survey! Timekeeping was easy with the railcar. The co-operative driver poses on the platform with the ETS in the hoop eager to get on to Arklow.

No 69 prepares to work out of a brightly illuminated Cork during the Michael Jackson concerts on the 23.00 to Cobh on Saturday 30 July 1988. The Mark 3 coach on the right, included in an Executive Cantrell & Cochrane 14.30 Special train from Dublin Heuston, has had the first class treatment – a set of orange curtains and "1" stickers on the windows, and perhaps the oily aisle carpet from the shunters boots has been cleaned! The C&C Special was the first one to return to Dublin on the Sunday morning departing at 00.01, arriving into Heuston at 02.40.

The driving cab end of Nos 737-68 railcar while working the 12.35 from Arklow at Wicklow over freshly dug out bullhead rails on Friday 30 September 1988. The small roundel cut in the gangway shutter was nicknamed 'The Porthole'. It was supposed to enable a second man, if he was tall enough, to see out through the folding back coach end window and shutter when acting as pilotman during single line working.

NIR Motive Power

The main staple of diesel motive power on NIR throughout the period covered by this book was undoubtedly the three members of Class 111. The first two entered service in February 1981, replacing the by-then unreliable Hunslets of 1970, and the third GM (No 113) in July 1984. Cross-border services, despite the seemingly constant interruptions of the Troubles, were at their fastest. The one hour fifty-nine minute timings of the non-stop trains in May 1984 became one hour fifty-five minutes from May 1985 up to June 1992 when they slipped a bit to one hour fifty-eight. Today, the timetable does not even have a non-stop service.

The next generation of locomotives arrived in May 1995 when Nos 208 and 209 appeared in their dark blue finery. There was a brief spell of fast running with them before the introduction of the De Dietrich coaches in September 1997, which relegated the cross-border timetable to a comparative trundle. Despite the 1997 launch aspirations of a one hour forty-five minute service, timings are now comparable with the steam timings of the late 1940's despite all that extra horsepower, signalling and technology.

The ill-fated purchase of the former Class C locomotives from CIÉ was a pity. The projected traffic flows did not materialise, and the aged equipment was already worn out and temperamental. Three of the locos (Nos 104/106/108) managed to give over seven years' service, No 109 managed almost seventeen months while No 107 lasted only nine months. On a railway system that was very well served by competent railcars, the locomotive-hauled trains were a welcome diversion, providing cross-border trains, which, despite the worst that circumstances could throw at them, still provided an excellent service.

The railbus, as it was known on NIR, is pictured here at Portadown on a special working, sporting a commemorative shield headboard for the official opening of the refurbished station on Friday 27 April 1984. The station had been badly damaged on 14 February 1982 when a bomb exploded near the booking office bringing down part of the roof. Normal train services were resumed the following morning with passengers using the entrance doors usually reserved for the off-loading Royal Mail road vans.

The BRE-Leyland R3 type railbus was built in 1981 by BREL at Derby (Litchurch Lane) and used as a demonstrator on British Rail, allocated the number RDB 977020. It also worked a regular service on the Western Region between Severn Beach and Bristol from October 1981 to May 1982. Before purchase by NIR it was exhibited on a lorry at the Royal Dublin Society Showground in 1981.

The number RB3 was given by NIR to the railbus but apparently it was never carried on the vehicle. It was re-gauged and was formally launched at York Road on Thursday 6 August 1982 with invited guests then travelling in the railbus at 12.15 for luncheon at the Dolphin Hotel, Whitehead. RB3 worked mostly on the Portrush branch plus occasional railtours and some inspection workings. It was withdrawn from service in December 1992 and then displayed for a while in the Railway Gallery of the Ulster Folk and Transport Museum at Cultra, Co Down. It is now on loan to the Downpatrick and Co Down Railway where it sees occasional service.

The painters are progressing well on former CIÉ Class C No 216, soon to become NIR No 104, in the works at Belfast York Road on Tuesday 21 January 1986. NIR at first leased six of these locomotives, and then purchased them outright in April 1986. Their intended use was on domestic waste traffic between Greencastle and Magheramorne and transport of lignite (low grade coal) to power stations, neither of which materialised. This locomotive had entered traffic in July 1957, and was fitted with a new General Motors engine at Inchicore in November 1971. It moved to NIR in December 1985, entering traffic as the first of Class MV in February 1986. It was scrapped at Hamill's scrap yard in Belfast's harbour estate in September 1997.

Paintwork complete, No 104 basks in the evening sun in the up sidings at the south end of Portadown station on Tuesday 1 July 1986. Initially Class MV was used mainly on Permanent Way trains, but later worked as Adelaide Yard pilot, placing cement wagons below the silos for discharging.

The wagons in this train are of interest. The yellow bogie ballast wagons are former BR Southern Region 18-ton 'Walrus' type, numbered in the 620XX series and had been built by the Southern Railway. NIR purchased eight in October 1983, numbering them C491–498. The third wagon is one of the former 20-ton, four-wheel, side-discharge spoil wagons of which seventy were built by Cravens of Sheffield in 1966 for the contract to haul stone from Magheramorne to Greencastle for construction of the M2 motorway.

NIR No 112 *Northern Counties* worked an 08.23 non-stop Budweiser Special Belfast Central–Dublin Connolly and then on to the Curragh for the Irish Derby on Saturday 27 June 1987. The Budweiser banners that were attached to the catwalk railings have long blown off and the stick-on headboards are looking the worse for wear. No 112 ran round its train at Dublin Connolly and, after reaching the Curragh main-line platform, it continued on to run round at Kildare. It then worked the empty stock back to Heuston for stabling where it is pictured, waiting to return with the empty carriages back to Kildare, prior to forming the 18.00 Curragh–Belfast. The ten coach NIR Mark 2 set included two dining cars (Nos 546/547), no doubt to dispense copious quantities of the train sponsor's brew! At that time it was very rare to see NIR stock at Heuston but later No 112 would be a regular performer all over the Irish Rail network.

No 101 *Eagle* and a train comprised of the July 1978-vintage silver-grey liveried Mark 2s stands in the Central Service Depot at Belfast between turns on Thursday 14 April 1988. The large pile of scrap in the background is on Queen's Quay awaiting loading into a ship for export. The platform ends of the former Belfast and County Down station were immediately beyond the concrete fence and in line with the pile of scrap. No 101 was stopped in April

1994 and after storage at the Central Service Depot, York Road and Adelaide Yard, it moved to the RPSI base at Whitehead on 16 June 2001, where it was eventually scrapped in January 2010. NIR had already removed the engine, traction motors and many other parts to keep No 102 going, leaving No 101 little more than a shell.

NIR No 112 *Northern Counties* runs round the 17.00 from Belfast Central at Dun Laoghaire on Monday 16 May 1988. A party of forty-one enthusiasts from the Modern Railway Society of Ireland was invited to travel on this inaugural run which returned as the 19.55 Dun Laoghaire–Belfast. This train was prominent in the new NIR timetable launched that day and aimed at cross-channel passengers using the Dun Laoghaire–Holyhead sea crossing. This lightly used service lasted until September 1990. It required Irish Rail conductor drivers and guards, and the run-round at Dun Laoghaire was awkward, having to be slotted in between DART services.

Mark 2F carriage NIR No 546 can be seen on the left. This was formerly BR M1800 RSS, (Restaurant Self Service), converted in 1974 at Derby Litchurch Lane from Mark 2F open second class coach No M5970 to serve as a prototype for catering facilities in the APT (Advanced Passenger Train). It was purchased by NIR in 1982.

Class MV No 108 (formerly CIÉ Class C No 230) in the running shed at York Road on Thursday 4 August 1988. Despite an introduction to service date of December 1987, it seems to have done little work, judging by the pristine paintwork. Hunslet No 102 *Falcon* is in the background, and on the far right, Class 450 three-car set No 452 *Olderfleet Castle* is receiving attention to its cylinder head gaskets. An end shutter door for a Class 80 driving trailer is propped up against the railbus on the right. The packing crates on the left are the type used for parts from General Motors, and were also used for movement of materials to and from Inchicore Works.

It was unusual to see the three Hunslets together, but my luck was in at the Central Service Depot on Saturday 21 January 1989. Nos 103 *Merlin*, 101 *Eagle* and 102 *Falcon* are lined up opposite the running shed. All three were introduced in July 1970 for cross-border services, working trains of Mark 2s in push-pull mode. Winter services were powered by one locomotive but the heavier summer services were often topped and tailed by two locomotives. No 103 was the first to be scrapped, at Ballymena in June 1997. No 102 is preserved at the Railway Gallery at the Cultra Museum, Co Down, arriving there in January 2012 after cosmetic restoration by the RPSI at Whitehead, Co Antrim, and painted in the original NIR maroon livery.

No 111 *Great Northern* stands at Dublin Connolly prior to working the 11.00 to Belfast Central on Saturday 20 May 1989. The second vehicle in the train is first class Mark 2F No 904 (formerly BR No 3367) purchased by NIR in 1988 and still in BR Inter-City livery. The third vehicle is Mark 2F dining car No 546.

Double-headed Hunslets Nos 102 *Falcon* and 103 *Merlin* depart from Dublin Connolly on the 13.00 to Belfast Central on Saturday 24 June 1989. This unusual motive power configuration resulted from failure of No 111 *Great Northern* the previous evening at Belfast. The pair hauled the 09.00 from Belfast that morning and this return working but No 111 was pronounced fit to work the 17.00 from Belfast and the 20.15 return later that evening. I came across this situation purely by chance, having travelled from Waterford that morning on the 07.40. Walking into Dublin Connolly to catch the 13.40 to Sligo, the distinctive sound of a Hunslet, never mind two, immediately caught my attention!

No 113 *Belfast & Co Down* poses at the site of the former Knockmore Junction while working a train for official publicity photographs on Sunday 9 July 1989. The Special left Belfast Central at 10.25 and posed for photographs here for 15 minutes, before running round at Ballinderry and returning to Lisburn. The train then worked to Poyntzpass, posing for twenty-five minutes at Knock Bridge just south of Portadown and, after running round at Poyntzpass returned to the Central Service Depot. Mark 2B first

class Executive saloon No 913 is next to the engine. This unusual vehicle had Mark 2D windows on the saloon side and regular sliding top-light windows on the corridor side. The saloon seated six first class passengers around a boardroom table and another six in a seating area. It could be hired for exclusive use for £55 including a dedicated steward, provided all passengers had a first class ticket! The other first class coaches in the photograph are Mark 2B No 901 (formerly NIR No 801) and Mark 2C No 903 (formerly BR FO No 3166, purchased by NIR in 1983).

No 101 *Eagle* failed just short of Adelaide while propelling the 16.55 from Bangor to Portadown on Sunday 22 April 1990. Sister locomotive No 102 was despatched from the Central Service Depot to push the failed train to Lisburn and clear the way for the following 18.00 to Dublin. Here No 102 is coupling up to the cement-begrimed No 101 to get the train on the move again. Fellow railway enthusiast Philip Martin can be seen in the fifth window of freshly painted 'micro buffet' coach No 548. He would probably have found a calendar of more use than his usual stopwatches on this occasion!

NIR 113 *Belfast & Co Down* is stabled with a fine 10-coach train of Mark 2s just off the southern end of Pearse Station platforms on Sunday 16 September 1990. A special timetable was in operation due to the two-week closure of the Dublin–Belfast line at Portadown for bridge renewal over the River Bann. Two NIR GMs (Nos 111 and 113), and fifteen NIR coaches were stabled on the southern side of these works.

The GAA All-Ireland Football Final was being played at Croke Park, bringing nine specials from Cork and one from Mallow. All ran to Dublin Connolly so every opportunity was taken to keep the platforms clear for the arriving specials leading to No 113 being in this unusual location, opposite the Boston Yard.

Class MV No 104 works a discharging ballast train between the platforms at Dunmurry on Sunday 30 June 1991. The Civil Engineering Department had possession of the up line at Dunmurry for the day to complete formation and drainage renewal works. No 104 was kept busy that day, working four return trains of hopper wagons between here and Fraser Street siding near the former Ballymacarrett Junction and Central Service Depot in Belfast. No 104 sports an Armagh-registered car number plate behind its left lamp bracket, presumably not a trophy! The patches on the cab front are the result of a collision with a wagon of rails, which were protruding over the end of a wagon.

The railbus tackles the climb of 1 in 100 past the single platform of the former Mountpleasant station on a return Civil Engineer's inspection train from Dundalk on Wednesday 17 July 1991. Use of the railbus for inspection work was ideal as there was easy access to the track through the wide driver operated doors. Also there was no need to run round or turn!

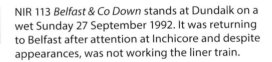

NIR 113 *Belfast & Co Down* stands at Dundalk on a wet Sunday 27 September 1992. It was returning to Belfast after attention at Inchicore and despite appearances, was not working the liner train.

CIÉ Class C No 224 stands derelict at the former narrow gauge platform at Ballymena in company with No 103 *Merlin* and fellow Class MV No 109 on Saturday 10 October 1992. No 224 was intended to become NIR 105 but inspection at York Road Works revealed twisted frames, so no work was done. Class C No 218 later replaced No 224, and took up the NIR number 105 as the last of the six to enter service in April 1991. No 224 was scrapped at Ballymena in January 1996 and No 103 was also cut up there the following June.

No 109 was brought from Ballymena to York Road to donate a bogie to, or swop one with, No 104 in November 1992. As No 105 needed the other bogie from No 109, it was decided in March 1993 to cut up the latter as in any case it had a seized engine. It was unusual to scrap locomotives inside the works at York Road; some parts were donated by NIR to the Irish Traction Group for their preserved Class C No 226 at Carrick on Suir, Co Tipperary.

Cement-dusted from its duties at Adelaide, No 101 *Eagle* prepares to shunt Great Southern Railways Class 800 4-6-0 No 800 *Maeve* onto the short siding at Cultra and into the Railway Gallery on Sunday 14 February 1993. This was part of the 'Big Move', the transferring of exhibits from Adelaide Yard to Cultra, Co Down.

Two trains were operated from Adelaide Yard, the first at 08.00 was formed by locomotives NIR No 113, steam locomotives Belfast & County Down Railway 4-4-2T No 30, and Great Northern Railway (Ireland) 2-4-2T No 93, and Dundalk Newry & Greenore Railway coach No 1, tailed by NIR No 101. This cavalcade took just over an hour for the journey

The second train departed from Adelaide at 12.00 led by NIR No 101 and comprised steam locomotives GSR 800 and LMS Northern Counties Committee 4-4-0 No 74 *Dunluce Castle* and tailed by NIR No 113. No 101 ran light engine from Central to Cultra siding. Its place was taken by RPSI ex GNR (I) 4-4-0 No 171 *Slieve Gullion* (in steam) and the cavalcade arrived at Cultra at 14.30, with No 113 acting as a (non-powered) brake van (although others might dispute this alleged division of labour). No 171 then ran light engine to Rockport Emergency Crossover and returned to Whitehead via Antrim, picking up its train of carriages at Belfast Central.

No 111 *Great Northern* scurries across the Curragh with the 12.35 empty carriage working from Kildare to Dublin Heuston for servicing on Sunday 27 June 1993. This nine-coach train had left Belfast Central at 09.00, with a special party of 300 for the Derby at the Curragh. The return working left the Curragh at 18.55, arriving Belfast Central at 22.00. The fifth vehicle from the engine is dining car No 547, now running in the RPSI Mark 2 train. The last three vehicles are all first class.

Another cross-border special on the same day left Belfast Central at 11.15 with 600 concert goers for the Red Hot Chilli Peppers in Dublin. The train was made up of a nine-car Class 80 set, returning from Connolly at 23.59; no first class required!

No 112 *Northern Counties* brings the 17.00 from Belfast Central to Dublin Connolly across Knockarney level crossing between Poyntzpass and Newry on Tuesday 31 August 1993. The demand for first class accommodation on the 09.00 and 17.00 workings from Belfast was less than with the 08.00 and the 15.00, with Nos 912 or 915 added to the tail of the train, providing just sixteen first class seats. Micro buffet No 548, formerly No 821, is the second coach from the rear; the catering area formerly occupied by two bays of four seats across the coach was denoted by a short red stripe above the window. In the background is the Portadown–Newry Canal while not far behind the photographer, is the track bed of the long-closed Goraghwood to Armagh line.

Class MV No 104 runs round its short train of three ballast wagons at Poyntzpass on Wednesday 9 March 1994. The Permanent Way Department was relaying the down line at the Border during an engineer's possession. No 104 and its train made three return trips, via Dundalk, to Poyntzpass for reloading. The bogie ballast wagons are part of a fleet of six, branded 'NIR Infrastructure Division', numbered C521–526, which had been built in France in 1993. Each weighs twenty-three tonnes with a load capacity of up to forty tonnes of ballast at a maximum speed of 50 mph.

No 112 *Northern Counties* arrives in Newry with the 13.00 Dublin Connolly–Belfast Central on Thursday 23 June 1994. The railwayman in charge can be seen leaving his portacabin, which contained the signalling equipment, booking office and a small kitchen. The draughty booking office window can be seen beside the door. The two 'darned-in' sleepers and length of rail in front of No 112 are a result of a bomb that exploded at 03.00 on 23 February 1990 badly damaging the previous portacabin and signalling equipment.

This set had been strengthened to accommodate 153 children from St Paul's High School, Newry on the 09.00 from Belfast Central. There is no sign yet of the Newry by-pass road, eventually to be part of the main Belfast to Dublin road which was constructed in the fields on the left of this picture.

Class MV No 108 heads the Irish Rail weed-spraying train at Lisburn on Thursday 23 June 1994. This train had worked all over the NIR system on a four day programme, the locomotive having run light engine to Dundalk to both collect and return the train. The NIR weekly notice contained the warning "staff to note the running of the spray train and to go to a place of safety on the passage of the train", the place of safety not being defined. There was no equivalent notice in the CIÉ circular – the striped headboards on the locomotive were obviously considered sufficient warning!

Crowds at the Curragh platform trying to board the return 18.00 Budweiser Special to Belfast on Sunday 26 June 1994. This short train for 120 first class passengers was headed by No 112 *Northern Counties* and was made up of coaches Nos 914/546/901/903/904 & 912. The second Special for Belfast at 18.55 was headed by No 113 *Belfast & Co Down* and was larger with eleven coaches, mostly booked by one party of 510 passengers.

No 113 *Northern Counties* gets away from Dundalk past the Central Cabin and Traffic Place with the 17.00 Belfast Central–Dublin Connolly on Wednesday 6 July 1994. The buildings on the right and left of the main line track are remnants of the old Dublin and Belfast Junction Railway station of 1848. The siding on the left at the former platform was still in regular use for making up liner trains for Adelaide. The other sidings on the left in the distance led to the former Irish North Western yard, part of which later became the new goods depot at Ardee Road when Barrack Street depot closed in March 1995.

Class MV No 108 shunts at Yorkgate with a train of the newer bogie ballast hopper wagons while No 459 *Killyleagh Castle* waits in the background on Friday 12 August 1994. No 108 had the honour of being the first NIR locomotive to work out onto the new cross harbour bridge with a loaded ballast train on 17 June 1994. No 459 is waiting to return to the platforms at Yorkgate, having just been the first railcar to have worked out to the centre of the Dargan Bridge on a test train.

No 113 *Belfast & Co Down* passes the site of the former signal cabin at Kellystown Summit between Dunleer and Drogheda with the 09.00 Belfast Central-Dublin on Saturday 17 September 1994. The bridge marks the end of the nine-mile climb from the Dunleer direction, and commencement of the five-mile descent towards Drogheda. A miniature signal cabin with only four levers was located on the up side embankment beside No 113. This was provided to break up the ten-mile long section between Drogheda North and Dunleer and improve the flow of traffic, mainly in conjunction with special workings. The cabin was last used around 1968/69 and formally closed on 13 June 1972.

Fairly clean No 111 *Great Northern* brings the 10.15 Belfast Central–Dublin Connolly past the Central Cabin at Dundalk on Sunday 19 March 1995. Unusually there are two generator vans together behind the locomotive; the first is No 913, the first class Executive Coach combined with Generator Van, easily identifiable by its different window profile.

Rationalisation works are in progress at Dundalk; the siding on the right has been lifted and the sleepers stacked in the right foreground while the other siding is clipped out of use and has gone rusty.

No 209, with No 208 in the background, undergo their start-up tests and pre-delivery inspections at the Inchicore running shed on Wednesday 5 April 1995. They had been unloaded from the delivery ship in Dublin on 24 and 25 March 1995 along with eleven members of the Class 201 for Iarnrod Éireann. No 209 travelled to York Road on 21 April with No 208 following the next day. No 208 entered traffic on 17 May but No 209 was delayed until 8 June 1995.

No 111 *Great Northern* brings the 17.00 Belfast Central–Dublin Connolly through the Lisburn Road suburbs of Belfast approaching the Lislea Drive footbridge on Tuesday 25 April 1995. The third line on the left ran parallel to the main lines between the crossover just on the Belfast side of Balmoral Halt as far as Adelaide Yard. A head shunt off the third line provided access to the Permanent Way depot and rail welding plant at Lislea Drive. At the Belfast end of Adelaide Yard, the third line was used to enable steam locomotives to travel to and from Great Victoria Street Station, free of the main line. Remnants of that line were in use as a headshunt to gain access to the Guinness yard.

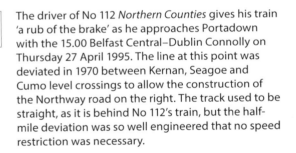

The driver of No 112 *Northern Counties* gives his train 'a rub of the brake' as he approaches Portadown with the 15.00 Belfast Central–Dublin Connolly on Thursday 27 April 1995. The line at this point was deviated in 1970 between Kernan, Seagoe and Cumo level crossings to allow the construction of the Northway road on the right. The track used to be straight, as it is behind No 112's train, but the half-mile deviation was so well engineered that no speed restriction was necessary.

The driver of No 112 *Northern Counties* has his hand on the black-handled train brake at Botanic while working the 15.00 Belfast Central–Dublin Connolly on Monday 1 May 1995. The platforms are unusually deserted as it is a Bank Holiday and train set working was returning to normal after a planned total line closure the previous day between Botanic and Adelaide. Installation of pointwork at Central Junction for the re-opening of Great Victoria Street Station required a considerable amount of work, as did the installation of the pointwork at City Junction to allow direct access to Great Victoria Street via the Blythfield Curve.

Pictured through an arch of the Donegall Road Bridge from Belfast City Hospital Halt, No 111 *Great Northern* travels slowly round the curve from Central Junction with the 11.00 from Dublin Connolly on Saturday 28 June 1997. The pointwork under Diner 546, the fourth coach in the train, leads to Great Victoria Street, round Blythfield curve. The first three vehicles in the train are all first class. Despite all the troubles and disruption to cross-border services, first class traffic stayed remarkably buoyant.

Class MV No 106 (formerly CIÉ Class C No 227) stands on a short piece of track beside the River Ferta at Cahirciveen, Co Kerry, on Thursday 11 June 1998 with the former railway bridge in the background. No 106 had been the longest in service with NIR (eight years and nine months) when it was stopped with major electrical problems in March 1995. It was the last operational member of the class.

As No C227 this engine had worked the last passenger train on 1 February 1960 when the thirty-nine mile branch from Farranfore to Valentia Harbour closed. A local heritage group in Cahirciveen purchased the locomotive for static display. It left Belfast by road on 8 October 1997 and was placed on the former track-bed beside the heritage centre. The locomotive was not in good condition following two years' outside storage at Belfast, with removal of parts (both authorised and unauthorised), and the attention of vandals. The plan was cosmetically to restore the locomotive at Cahirciveen, paint it in the original silver livery and with the number 227. These plans were not

realised and the locomotive was further vandalised; scrapping was suggested in August 2005 as it was becoming an eyesore.

No 106 was removed from Cahirciveen in April 2007 by a preservation group and is currently in store at Kilmacow, Co Waterford, painted silver but numbered incorrectly as 202.

No 113 *Belfast & Co Down* takes the former Great Southern & Western route through Glasnevin Junction with a 09.00 Special from Belfast Central for the Irish Derby at the Curragh on Sunday 28 June 1998. The track on the extreme right is the former Midland Great Western line from the North Wall to link with that company's route from the Broadstone Station to the west at Liffey Junction. The line from Glasnevin Junction to the North Wall and Connolly Station via Newcomen Junction had been temporarily closed since May 1998, for the construction of the enlarged stadium at Croke Park, which created a railway tunnel under the stand at the Canal End.

NIR Railcars

The 'railcars' as they were always known in Ireland, had a long pedigree, back to those pioneering passenger efforts on the Castlederg and Victoria Bridge Tramway and the Clogher Valley Railway. Henry Forbes on the County Donegal Railway later greatly improved upon the genre, with the ever-helping hand of the Great Northern at Dundalk in the background. The GNR(I) were the pioneers of Irish railcars on a larger scale, and pre-war experience particularly with railcars D, E and F led to the introduction of a considerable fleet of AEC sets in 1950.

The Ulster Transport Authority continued the modernisation programme in the early 1950s, constructing Multi Engined Diesel (MED) and Multi Purpose Diesel (MPD) railcars. After the break-up of the Great Northern Railway Board (successor to the GNR) in 1958, the UTA inherited half the latter's fleet of modern diesel railcars that had been built by Associated Equipment Company (AEC), British United Traction (BUT) and at Dundalk Works.

When formed in April 1967, NIR inherited a variety of this stock just as the last of the eight members of Class 70 were entering service. The first significant investment by the Northern Ireland Government in NIR was in July 1970 when the three new Hunslet Locomotives and coaches released Class 70 from cross-border work for other duties, mainly on the old LMS NCC section. The need to replace ageing and increasingly unreliable AEC/BUT railcars, and a revival of Government interest in rail transport led to placement of an order in 1972 for nine Class 80 railcar sets, with delivery two years later. The announcement of the Belfast Central project confirmed official confidence in NIR, and a further thirteen Class 80 sets were ordered in 1975.

Other than the arrival of the ex-BREL railbus in August 1982, there were no further additions to the power car railcar fleet until October 1985. Between then and June 1987, the eight creaking Class 70 were replaced by nine Class 450 sets. These vehicles together with Class 80 soldiered on, despite the numerous malicious attacks, until Class 3000 arrived from Spain in 2004, followed by Class 4000 from the same builder (Compania Auxiliare de Ferrocarriles) in 2011.

Overall, Classes 70 and 80 provided excellent and reliable service, their multiple working (within class) capacity permitting flexibility in set length as traffic levels demanded. They were designed for ease of use for drivers, guards and engineering staff and well capable of handling all that was required of them.

Newly out-shopped Class 80 power car No 84, in the-then latest livery, rests on the turntable at Belfast York Road surrounded by works accommodation bogies on Thursday 22 March 1984. Sister power car No 81 in the new livery worked the special train for the opening of the new Newry station in May 1984.

This was effectively the public launch of the new livery despite it having been in service for two months. Railcar livery had remained unchanged since the introduction of Class 80 in 1974, and the next change followed the 1988 sectorisation into 'Suburban' and 'Inter-City' divisions. The first vehicle to appear in the new suburban livery was again No 84, in February that year, and the first Inter-City liveried vehicle was power car No 96 named *Glenshane* in September 1988.

On Monday 14 May 1984 the 'new' Newry station, constructed on the site of the former Bessbrook station closed in 1942, was opened in response to a local campaign. Nos 81-763-753, complete with commemorative headboard arrived with the opening 11.07 special from Belfast. Most of the congratulatory speeches for the 200-odd guests, and much hand shaking took place at Portadown station, as the facilities at Newry were limited. The new station proved very successful and has since undergone at least three upgrades. The most recent buildings are palatial compared to the first shelters and temporary 'hut' style waiting rooms. Customs inspection for Belfast-bound trains was transferred from Portadown to a hut for the Customs men on the platform.

No 81 had been badly damaged in a bomb explosion at Broomhedge between Lisburn and Moira on 21 May 1976; the passenger saloon was eventually rebuilt at Derby, returning to service in June 1978.

The black platform gates are closed as Class 70 Nos 75 *River Maine* and 77 *River Braid* call at Dundalk for customs examination on Thursday 31 May 1984. The empty set from the Central Service Depot in Belfast was running to Mosney to collect a returning party of children from St Brigid's High School in Armagh, departing from Mosney at 17.30 for Portadown. The original plan had been to attach a three-car Class 80 set to the rear of the 14.05 from Belfast Central, departing Portadown at 15.00 as empty carriages for Mosney.

In the background No 164 shunts wagons of Harp Lager kegs from the brewery loading bank, just out of sight on the right. All the sidings have long since been removed to provide car parking for the large number of commuters who travel to Dublin.

The main line signal is off at Mullingar on Tuesday 30 July 1985 for an NIR Special of 1000 Scouts heading for a ten-day-long Jamboree at Portumna, Co Galway. The train started as a three-car (known locally as a three-piece) set from Bangor at 06.45, and called at Holywood and Belfast Central, where its size was increased to twelve vehicles. Further pick-up stops were made between Central and Newry. Arrival at Ballinasloe was at 12.35. The empty carriages returned to Belfast at 13.30 running non-stop to Dublin Connolly via Moate. Other CIÉ specials to Ballinasloe on the same day included two from Dublin Connolly and one from Sligo. The first Special

from Connolly at 07.25 required a special DART connecting train from Bray at 06.20. Two special trains of scouts also ran from Dublin Heuston to Roscrea, the first departing at 06.45.

The 450 Castle Class used new bodies mounted on second-hand Mark 1 carriage underframes built by BREL at Derby, with refurbished engines and electrical equipment recovered from the withdrawn Class 70 power cars. They earned the nickname '66,000 cc shopping trolleys' after an unfortunately catchy Suburban advertising campaign. They were never sparkling performers and their basic, uncomfortable interiors made them unpopular with passengers, especially on longer journeys over the former NCC main line. Just out of the box Class 450 trailers Nos 781 and 791 are pictured in the running shed at Belfast York Road on Thursday 22 August 1985. The trailers had yet to be matched with power car No 451 *Belfast Castle*. No 451 was first of the nine sets, entering traffic in October 1985 and it was the first set to be stopped in January 2011, and cut up at Belfast York Road in April 2012.

The Class 450 was launched in a blaze of publicity at York Road on Monday 28 October 1985 when, according to the *Belfast Telegraph*, Secretary of State, Tom King "drove off in the *Belfast Castle*". We can only presume that he returned to launch *Olderfleet Castle* on the same day.

Displaying a very upmarket headboard reading "We were the champions" Nos 75 *River Maine*-728-77 *River Braid* are ready for the departure of an RPSI-organised 'farewell special' from Londonderry Waterside on Saturday 12 October 1985. The train had covered the ninety-three miles non-stop from Belfast York Road in eighty-four minutes, an excellent performance from a set originating in 1966 and shortly due for withdrawal. The return to Belfast Central was more leisurely, including photographic stops at Downhill and main stations from there to Antrim.

With its *River Braid* nameplate removed, hopefully for safe keeping, No 77 has arrived at Dublin Connolly with the delayed 17.00 from Belfast Central on Thursday 5 December 1985. The set was made up from the remaining serviceable Class 70 vehicles (Nos 77-728-724-725-721-75) and this was the last visit of the type to Dublin.

A nationwide teachers' strike had been announced for 5 December and the teachers' trade union organised a rally at Croke Park requiring four large specials to Heuston and three more to Connolly. With this extra demand coinciding with the traditionally busiest pre-Christmas shopping day, NIR had been requested to provide extra stock for cross-border services in order to release a CIÉ Mark 2 set for a special from Ballina.

This Class 70 set was withdrawn on Monday 3

February 1986 to donate its engine and electrical equipment to new Class 450. However, due to continuing heating and ventilation problems with the new class it was re-instated in mid February. While working a return Junior Orangeman's Special from Larne to Belfast on Easter Tuesday 1 April 1986, the set was badly vandalised necessitating its immediate and permanent withdrawal on arrival at Belfast York Road.

The Foyle Valley Railway Society organised a 05.45 special train from Londonderry to Cork for 800 soccer supporters to watch Derry play Cork on Sunday 16 March 1986. The twelve-piece Class 80 set was made up with power cars Nos 81/85/68/97, and presented an impressive sight. Arrival at Cork, just after 14.00, was seventy-four minutes late, mainly due to permanent way works and malicious emergency cord pulling at Connolly. The return departure at 18.29 was nine minutes late and more permanent way delays were encountered around Malahide and Skerries. Further delay was incurred at Ballymena through crossing a late running empty carriage working from Derry. Arrival at Derry was one hour late – at 02.40 the following morning.

In this picture, the set is passing the signal cabin at Cork and approaching the platform to start loading for the return journey.

Painters in the shops at Belfast York Road were getting fed up with the changes to the new Suburban sector livery. This variant on driving trailer No 739 on Friday 8 January 1988 thankfully did not make it into service. The white and orange stripes were later lowered to clear the window frames. The first set in the new corrected colours, Nos 84-768-739, entered service on 10 February 1988.

Needing power car No 93 in service urgently, it was released from York Road Workshops before the number, logo and the warning diamond could be applied to the front end. It is pictured between turns inside the running shed at the Central Service Depot at Queens Quay, Belfast on Thursday 14 April 1988. This vehicle was badly burned in an orgy of destruction at Lurgan on 6 July 1997 together with No 82. Both power cars were sent to Railcare at Glasgow for repairs, but the four intermediate trailers of the train were not so fortunate as all went for scrap. No 93 returned to service in October 1999 and was scrapped at Ballymena in February 2012.

Class 80 sets travelled quite extensively away from their home ground, mainly on specials. When three sets were hired by Irish Rail, the increased drivers' route knowledge helped them reach quite remote locations! A nine-piece set composed of power cars Nos 92/95/67 worked from Portadown at 07.55 to Claremorris, for Knock Shrine pilgrims on Thursday 12 May 1988.

Travel time for the 229-mile journey via Connolly, Portarlington and Athlone was just under five hours on the way out, and five and a quarter hours on the return. The twenty minutes extra on the return journey were required to cross two trains at Clara and Tullamore on the branch. The train was unusually Customs cleared at Dublin Connolly before departure. It later ran as empty carriages from Portadown to the Central Service Depot in Belfast.

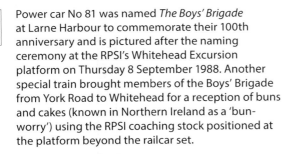

Power car No 81 was named *The Boys' Brigade* at Larne Harbour to commemorate their 100th anniversary and is pictured after the naming ceremony at the RPSI's Whitehead Excursion platform on Thursday 8 September 1988. Another special train brought members of the Boys' Brigade from York Road to Whitehead for a reception of buns and cakes (known in Northern Ireland as a 'bun-worry') using the RPSI coaching stock positioned at the platform beyond the railcar set.

No 95 has unusual company in the running shed at the Central Service Depot in Belfast on Sunday 19 February 1989. There had been a spell of lengthy bomb scares at various locations between Dundalk and Lurgan, which stranded rolling stock away from their respective home depots. CIÉ Nos 074/144/181 were stabled in the depot until the scares ended. The previous day all cross-border trains had been cancelled including the 07.55 Belfast Central–Dublin Connolly Special for the Ireland vs England match at Lansdowne Road, which would have used a twelve vehicle Class 80 set.

The War Memorial at Belfast York Road has a backdrop of three Class 450 sets on St Patrick's Day, Saturday 17 March 1990. The War Memorial was erected by the Midland Railway (Northern Counties Committee), and was unveiled on Thursday 24 November 1921. When York Road Station closed in October 1992, the Memorial was moved into storage.

No 97 receives some final spit and polish at Belfast York Road before departing for its naming ceremony on Monday 30 April 1990. Nos 97 and 99 worked a special train at 10.25 comprising Inter-City liveried, fully tabled stock to Ballymoney where No 97 was named *Glenshesk* after one of the nine glens of Antrim. The four-car set later worked empty to Coleraine to stable before returning to Ballymoney to bring the invited dignatories back to York Road on a 16.26 special. The covered-up nameplate can be seen on the bodyside. No 99 had previously been named *Sir Myles Humphries* in September 1978 after the then NIR Chairman.

Busy day at Scarva on Saturday 13 July 1991, the day of the annual Sham Fight (a re-enactment of the 1690 Battle of the Boyne) at the Co Down village. Over 2000 members of the Royal Black Preceptory travelled in six special trains departing from Portadown between 10.00 and 11.15. Return trains from Scarva started at 15.30, trains leaving at ten-minute intervals. A large number of the general public travelled as well. Here we can see a return special tailed by No 89 departing for Portadown while No 90 passes with empty carriages from Portadown to Poyntzpass to cross over and form a later return working from Scarva to Portadown.

To the left is the topiary figure of 'Old Bill', complete with Orange Sash. He has since succumbed, perhaps with box blight! In the right foreground is the base of the former water tower while further back cars are parked on the former bay platform for Banbridge trains.

The staff at Belfast York Road cleaned trains at the platforms using the traditional long-handled brush and a bucket of Exmover, with a final hose down to remove the residue. The result always seemed better than that achieved by the train wash at the Central Service Depot. Here we can see a sparkling Class 450 No 453 *Moiry Castle* in Suburban livery at York Road Platform 1 on Wednesday 21 August 1991. No 453 entered service in December 1985 and was stopped in December 2011. After a period of storage on the middle road at Bangor, it was cut into sections at Adelaide Yard in May 2013 and removed by road to a scrap yard near Ballymena for final disposal.

A rather melancholy scene at the Central Service Depot in Belfast on the afternoon of Saturday 29 February 1992. The two Peace Trains stand side-by-side waiting to return from Belfast Central to Connolly at 17.25 and 18.10. That morning, one train had departed from Portadown at 06.10 and the other from Belfast Central at 06.40, both bound for Dublin Connolly. They then formed 09.50 (express) and 10.15 (stopping at main stations) return specials from Dublin to Belfast on which 1250 passengers travelled for a peace rally at Belfast City Hall.

The trains were seen off from Dublin by the Lord Mayor and a band, and welcomed in Belfast by dignitaries and yet another band. The trains were planned by The Peace Train Organisation, and their publicity flyer urged people to "Support the people and traders of Belfast"

The final train to leave from Belfast York Road was Class 450 set Nos 454 *Carrickfergus Castle*-794-784 on the 22.00 to Larne Harbour on Friday 16 October 1992, thus ending 144 years of history. A special headboard was displayed in the cab window, and a group of railway enthusiasts travelled out as far as Carrickfergus on the last train, returning on the last passenger working into York Road. The new station at nearby Yorkgate opened the following morning with the 06.45 to Larne Harbour.

Not the usual thing that you would expect to see at Ennis on a Sunday afternoon! The NIR set was on a special working from Newry for a GAA match between Counties Down and Clare at Ennis on Sunday 28 February 1993. A small party of Modern Railway Society of Ireland enthusiasts also travelled from Portadown where the empty stock originated. The railcars worked empty from Ennis to Limerick and return for fuel and servicing, providing the travelling enthusiasts with a photo stop at Sixmilebridge. Journey time from Newry to Ennis was around five hours including reversals at Dublin Connolly and Limerick.

No 160 is working the newly-introduced 16.45 service to Limerick, which arrived there at 17.25, and gave a connection into the 17.40 (direct) to Dublin Heuston. The empty carriages to form the 16.45 worked out from Limerick at 15.45, and had twenty minutes to run round after arrival.

No 83 sits on narrow gauge accommodation bogies at the ABB Litchurch Lane works in Derby on Thursday 25 March 1993. The power car passenger saloon was seriously damaged in a firebomb attack at Finaghy station on Thursday 20 August 1992 while working the 15.28 Lisburn–Bangor. The vehicle left for Derby in early 1993 and returned to NIR on 23 December 1993. Delivery from Derby was via Larne Harbour, when Class DL No 102 hauled No 83 to York Road. BR Mark 2C Second Open coach No M5586 was used to provide a source of spare parts for No 83, which re-entered service on 4 February 1994 with a slightly darker shade of blue paint.

The Central Service Depot (CSD), built in the former Queen's Quay station yard, Belfast, on Saturday 17 April 1993. CSD was closed in late November 1994 when the cross-harbour Dargan Bridge opened. The site was to be entirely buried under a series of new link roads between the bridges over River Lagan and the main Belfast to Bangor road. There are five

Class 80 sets around the yard and the one Class 450 set is at the fuelling point. The spare cross-border stock and GM locomotive are stabled in a siding at Fraser Street footbridge in the distance. On the left, alongside the boundary fence, Class MV No 104 and Class DL No 102 *Falcon* can also be seen.

An international Scout Jamboree at nearby Ballyfin required a five-car Class 80 special from Belfast to Portlaoise on Monday 26 July 1993. The train, (powered by Nos 92 and 81) departed from Central at 10.20, arriving at Portlaoise at 13.45, returning empty to Belfast at 13.50. The Scouts returned to Belfast on Friday 6 August, using another Class 80 set (powered by Nos 93 and 85). Other Scout specials on the same day included one each from Dublin Heuston and Cork. No 080 is arriving at the up platform with the 11.20 from Cork while the Scouts unload all their equipment from the guard's van of No 81.

Dundalk Stationmaster Brendan McQuaid is out and about checking his area of responsibility. He watches from the usually switched-out signal cabin at Dunleer as a six-piece Class 80 set including Nos 95 and 91 thunder through with empty carriages from Mosney to Portadown on Thursday 23 June 1994. The set had earlier worked a 09.25 special from Belfast Central for a group of 250 children who later returned back to Belfast at 17.40 in a three-piece 80 Class set headed by No 90. Dunleer cabin had less than three years of service left, closing on 17 May 1997 when the new signalling was commissioned

This was quite a busy day on NIR; a large day return Sunday School excursion from Londonderry to Portrush required a nine-piece Class 80 set. The spare GM loco and carriages headed by No 111 *Great Northern* worked several trains including an evening turn to Londonderry, to free up stock for the specials.

Class 450 set with No 458 *Antrim Castle* departs Whitehead with the 17.35 from Larne Harbour to Belfast Central on Wednesday 10 August 1994. This set started from Portadown at 06.20 that morning, running to Bangor, then to Lisburn and back to York Road for three hours of servicing. It then worked two return trips to Larne and one to Whitehead in the afternoon, finishing at 18.45. Total rostered mileage for the day was 206, perhaps not the most intensive use of rolling stock!

This set (458-798-788) is now preserved in running order at Downpatrick entering service there on 18 October 2014.

The honour of the first railcar to travel from Yorkgate out onto the cross-harbour line fell to No 459 *Killyleagh Castle* on Friday 12 August 1994. No 459 travelled very slowly, just as far as the middle of the Dargan Bridge for clearance tests, returning back to Yorkgate shortly afterwards. The lower picture is of No 459 pausing just outside Yorkgate on the return journey. The railcar on the left later worked to Whitehead, allowing the temporary red stop-block warning light to be manually lowered admitting No 459 back to the platforms at Yorkgate. The signal posts at the platform ends are wired and ready to receive their signal heads.

A Class 80 set departs from Belfast Central towards Bangor as No 454 *Carrickfergus Castle* stands on the centre of the Dargan Bridge in the background on Thursday 24 November 1994. The fire brigade were testing safe evacuation procedures with No 454, which is why the doors are open, and later used a road-mounted crane to test accessibility, parked on Donegall Quay below the bridge. The cross-harbour line opened for public timetabled service four days later, on 28 November 1994. The official opening took place on 9 March 1995 when HM Queen Elizabeth formally opened the road and rail bridges. A special platform was constructed to enable boarding of a Royal Train comprising sparkling Nos 455 *Galgorm Castle* and 459 *Killyleagh Castle* uniquely formed as a four-piece set for the short journey to Belfast Central.

No 90 stands in the new running shed at Belfast York Road on the evening of Thursday 30 March 1995. The shed was a vast improvement on those it replaced at the Central Service Depot and at York Road. There was a useful low-level inspection pit between the rails accessed by a few steps (edged in yellow in the foreground). Examination of bogies, brake gear and wheelsets was made much easier as they were now at eye level. Lighting in the pit shining upwards towards the underside of the vehicles was a far cry from the pit at CSD, which could not be used in certain tidal conditions due to flooding from the nearby River Lagan!

Major adjustment to the trackwork layout at Central Junction between Belfast Central and Adelaide for the re-opening of Great Victoria Street, required the diversion of Derry and Portrush trains via the then little-used Bleach Green Junction to Antrim section for a few days around the end of March 1995. Here we can see Nos 98 and 87 tackling the stiff climb past the disused up platform at Mossley while working the 10.06 Botanic–Portrush on Friday 31 March. The normally unattended, guard-operated, level crossings in this section were specially manned by the permanent way department to enable maintenance of a reasonable timetable, subject to the maximum 40 mph speed limit. The first few down trains to tackle the 1 in 76 climb from Bleach Green Junction to Monkstown had considerable problems with wheelslip due to poor rail conditions.

Gormanston reverberates as No 89 heads a nine-piece 10.25 special carrying 600 Annaghmore GAA supporters from Portadown to Dublin Connolly on Sunday 30 April 1995. This was the first of two specials from Portadown that morning – No 111 *Great Northern* departed at 10.50 with a relief to the regular Sunday morning train. Over 1200 supporters travelled on the two trains.

No 89 was the first Class 80 railcar to enter service on Saturday 5 October 1974 and the last passenger workings of the class took place in September 2011. No 89 itself was stopped in late 2010, and stored at Ballymena where it still resides in mid 2015. The Sandite railhead treatment train is formed of Class 80 vehicles painted bright yellow, so in the winter months it is still possible to hear the thump of the 4SRKT engine.

A smoky No 86 is notched up and gently rejoins the double track section at the saltmines near Kilroot while working the 18.00 Larne Town–Belfast Central on Wednesday 2 August 1995.

Due to constant coastal erosion in this area, the line was singled between here and Whitehead in August 1994 with trains working over the down line. The pointwork was installed in November 1994 and trains continued to work over the down line

and through Whitehead tunnel until a temporary diversion seaward around the tunnel became permanent in November 1997.

The long jetty at Cloghan Point in the distance is used by ships discharging oil to the Northern Ireland Electricity storage depot marked by the tall chimney, beside the line in the left background. On the right, the concrete building was one of two searchlight towers, which together with a big gun, were part of the protection of Belfast Lough during the Second World War.

Cross-border visits of the Class 450 were not as frequent as their Class 80 cousins. Here No 452 *Olderfleet Castle* eases past the Central Cabin in Dundalk during a shunt prior to forming the 20.20 to Bangor on Tuesday 21 May 1996.

Preparatory work has been carried out on the cabin prior to the 'Big Lift' which took place on 23 May. The signalman's toilet has already been demolished – let us hope he did not forget! – and note holes cut in the brickwork to receive the straps to lift the creaking wooden structure. The cabin was stored on a truck in the nearby Ardee goods yard before installation in preserved state on the island platform at Dundalk.

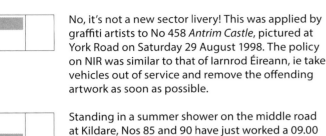

No, it's not a new sector livery! This was applied by graffiti artists to No 458 *Antrim Castle*, pictured at York Road on Saturday 29 August 1998. The policy on NIR was similar to that of Iarnrod Éireann, ie take vehicles out of service and remove the offending artwork as soon as possible.

Standing in a summer shower on the middle road at Kildare, Nos 85 and 90 have just worked a 09.00 Curragh race-goers Special from Belfast on Sunday 27 June 1999. The train originated in Great Victoria Street as the line was closed for an extended period between Central Junction and Belfast Central to allow for complete renewal of the track, signalling

and drainage. Enterprise services were diverted from Central Station to Great Victoria Street where special facilities were installed for the overnight stabling of stock. The return special to Belfast departed from the Curragh at 18.48, arriving back in Belfast at 21.50.

Other specials for the Curragh included two push-pull workings from Heuston, and a 09.05 special from Cork. When the Cork special returned home that evening, the empty set of carriages worked to Waterford at 01.30, arriving there at 04.00 to form the Monday morning 'Earlybird' to Heuston at 05.10. I am sure the gatekeepers between Limerick Junction and Waterford were pleased!

On the footplate

I was extremely fortunate to be granted footplate passes for my twice-yearly 'big ticket' tours of Irish Rail. The passes were initially granted for the period of the 'Rambler' tickets, as they were then known, which were valid for eight or fifteen consecutive days and available on all ordinary rail services. The fare for these eight days of unlimited travel in August 1982 was IE£42.00. On one Rambler ticket I managed to travel on the footplate of thirty-two different engines of five different classes and covered 2504 miles – quite good value.

There was always much to see and learn from the footplate. The drivers were most informative and usually very interested in their railway. I enjoyed many stories and tall tales, often about drivers and guards long retired. These experiences were of great value in the preparation of railtour brochures for the RPSI and MRSI.

Pictured from the rear cab on Monday 9 July 1984, summer rain falls at 10.03 as Nos 135 and 121 on the 07.50 from Westport cross No 086 on the 08.20 Dublin Heuston–Westport in the Clonnydonnin loop on the 22-mile single line section between Athlone and Tullamore. This route was particularly busy between 09.00 and 10.00, as both the up and down Westport and Galway trains all crossed and any late running could lead to substantial delays. Trains could be crossed at Tullamore, Clara, Clonnydonnin, and Athlone. Crews of crossing trains also exchanged footplates, usually at Athlone. Westport and Galway drivers exchanged footplates with Inchicore drivers, usually after a brief cup of tea. Some Athlone drivers worked right through to Dublin Heuston, returning with mid-morning trains.

The view from the cab of No 122 as the signalman comes down the steps of the signal cabin at Ballymote with the Electric Train Staff (ETS) for the section to Sligo on Wednesday 11 July 1984. Crossing Nos 122 and 130 on my train (the 08.30 from Dublin Connolly) was No 039 on a special train of palletised bagged cement wagons from Sligo to Drogheda via Dublin North Wall. The Sligo based driver of No 039 has stopped his short train with the locomotive as near as possible to the cabin to save the signalman a walk with the staff for the section to Boyle. This locomotive is now preserved in working order by the Irish Traction Group at Downpatrick, Co Down.

It's all go at Athlone on Sunday 16 August 1987. The cab door of No 083 is open as the Inchicore-based driver prepares to leave his footplate on the 09.20 Dublin Heuston–Galway. He will return to Dublin with No 077, which is arriving with the 10.05 Galway-Dublin Heuston. No 152 is the Athlone pilot in the left background, and No 081 idles awaiting departure with the 11.15 Athlone–Westport. This locomotive with its Mark 2 coach set had left Westport at 09.00 that morning, running as far as Athlone to provide a connection for passengers from Mayo to the Dublin–Galway route. On arrival back at Westport 13.10, No 081 will run round and form the 17.55 to Dublin Heuston.

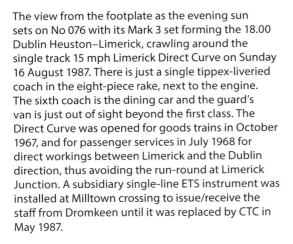

The view from the footplate as the evening sun sets on No 076 with its Mark 3 set forming the 18.00 Dublin Heuston–Limerick, crawling around the single track 15 mph Limerick Direct Curve on Sunday 16 August 1987. There is just a single tippex-liveried coach in the eight-piece rake, next to the engine. The sixth coach is the dining car and the guard's van is just out of sight beyond the first class. The Direct Curve was opened for goods trains in October 1967, and for passenger services in July 1968 for direct workings between Limerick and the Dublin direction, thus avoiding the run-round at Limerick Junction. A subsidiary single-line ETS instrument was installed at Milltown crossing to issue/receive the staff from Dromkeen until it was replaced by CTC in May 1987.

The shock of seeing the former Midland Great Western/Sligo Leitrim & Northern Counties railways joint loco shed at Sligo freshly demolished prompted me to grab this photograph from the footplate of

No 124 as it arrived in company with No 131 on the 13.40 from Dublin Connolly on Saturday 18 June 1988. The home signal that has been pulled 'off' is for the arrival platform, the other on the bracket is for the goods yard at Sligo Quay.

Bouncing along the Ballina branch in notch six on the footplate of No 192 with Claremorris Driver Martin Loughnane, while working the 13.30 Ballina–Manulla Junction on Friday 10 February 1989. The ETS for this section can be seen in the exchanging hoop hanging from the central vigilance button. These locomotives, like all on CIÉ, could be driven from either side with the deadman's foot pedal duplicated accordingly. By keeping the vigilance button depressed, the driver could change sides without activating the brakes automatically.

Simultaneous departures at Limerick Junction, as seen from the driver's side footplate of No 020. This locomotive is reversing the 15.35 Limerick–Rosslare Harbour round the back of the Junction towards Keane's Points as a Class 121 departs with the 15.00 up Day Mail from Cork to Dublin on Thursday 22 June 1989. The single Cravens coach next to the engine of the mail was for passengers, and a very pleasant way to travel to Dublin Heuston, provided you were not in a hurry.

The Park Royal and Cravens coaches plus the van on the rear of the Mail had been added at the Junction by No 020 and were being worked empty from Limerick back to Dublin. These Limerick-based passenger vehicles were probably returning to Inchicore for attention or routine examination.

A busy scene at Killarney, witnessed from the footplate of No 081 as it backs in with the 13.35 Tralee–Dublin Heuston on Sunday 16 June 1991. The GAA Munster Football Final between Kerry and Cork was being played at Fitzgerald Park Stadium, which used to have a platform just on the Tralee side of Killarney. There were seven specials for the match,

08.50 from Heuston, 09.00, 09.25, 09.50, 10.15 and 10.50 all from Cork, as well as an 11.45 special service from Tralee. A total of 3169 passengers travelled on the specials. The busiest train of the morning was the 09.50, with a loading of 721 Cork supporters – mighty stuff! Space at Killarney was very limited; No 077 and train was stabled in the headshunt outside Killarney, and a train of air-braked Mark 2 coaches was stabled in Tralee. A repeat would be impossible in 2015 as most of Killarney yard is now occupied by a shopping centre.

The view back from the footplate of No 144 with the weed-spray train in 'The-Dip' below the Belfast line, where the route from Church Road Junction to North Strand Junction goes under the former GNR(I) main line. No 080 is arriving with the 11.00 from Belfast Central on Tuesday 23 June 1992. The spray train was working its way back to Portlaoise Depot for replenishment, having sprayed the Athenry–Tuam, and Athenry–Mullingar sections the previous day.

 Vegetation has almost completely taken over the New Ross branch, near Glenmore, as this view from the cab of No 173 working the weed-spray train on Tuesday 30 June 1992 shows. It was a challenge to reach New Ross on this occasion as the train stalled less than half a mile from Abbey Junction. Despite using every trick including manual sanding, restarting proved impossible. The guard walked back to Abbey Junction and the train reversed back to Waterford station. After the passing of the Summer Only 12.45 Waterford–Rosslare Harbour, we again charged the bank, having retained the large ETS, and managed to get up that first mile of 1 in 60. We arrived in New Ross having been whacked by every sapling and bush along the way. Arriving safely back at Abbey Junction, we had to wait for the passing at 16.25 of No 150 on the 15.15 return working from the Harbour.

No 054 brings the 15.00 Bell Liner into Waterford from Dublin past No 160 which has just arrived with the 19.40 from Rosslare Harbour on Thursday 1 July 1993. No 054 had arrived in the Sally Yard around 19.30, and waited until No 160 and its short train cleared the Wellington Bridge–Abbey Junction

section before proceeding. The containers were worked to the Bell Lines yard at the Frank Cassin Wharf, which was replaced on 8 September 1993 by the new port at Belview further down the River Suir.

The view through the cab door of Nos 182 and 164 leaving the up loop at Kildare while working an 08.45 Community Games Special from Galway to Mosney on Saturday 27 August 1994. A following up train can just be discerned in the distance waiting at signals.

The empty carriages to form the special had run from Athlone at 06.30 that morning.

There were three specials for the 1994 games at Mosney: 08.10 from Ennis, 08.50 from Cork and the Galway Special. Return specials worked the following Tuesday 3 April to Ennis and Cork but the 273 passengers for Galway were accommodated on regular services.

End of the Line

On stopping work, most locomotives were stored at Inchicore pending formal withdrawal. There might follow a long interval before cutting up took place, especially if others of the same class remained in service, as those stored could be cannibalised for spare parts. Occasionally, an instruction was issued to cancel further work on a locomotive that was receiving minor finishing repairs after painting etc. Thus a locomotive in apparently pristine condition could be moved direct from the Works to the Inchicore scrap line where it presented an incongruous spectacle. Cutting up was also undertaken at Mullingar, Dundalk and in the Dublin North Wall Yard.

At Mullingar, a line of Class 401 (E) Nos 403, 408 and 402 await their fate on Friday 26 August 1988. All three had entered service in late 1957 and Nos 402 and 403 were stopped in early 1977, while No 408 soldiered on until mid-1983. Cutting up finally started in April 1989 close to the Bretland gantry on the down side of the former main line, beside Mullingar West signal box. The 500 ft long gantry supported an overhead crane that had been erected by the MGWR in 1923 to facilitate assembly of pre-fabricated track panels that were laid using the Bretland Tracklaying Train. The 'X' daubed on the locomotive side indicated that scrapping had been authorised, whereas 'V' applied in similar fashion noted scrapping requested. Conversion to the 'X' was quickly effected by adding on an upside down 'V'! These locos are standing beside the former locomotive shed, now a working base for the Railway Preservation Society of Ireland. The former Midland Great Western Railway main line to Athlone and points west is in the foreground.

The end cometh for Class A Nos 041 and 044 as their remains litter the scrap bank at Inchicore Works on Saturday 8 August 1992. Both entered service in May 1956 and both were withdrawn on Friday 5 October 1984 together with six others of this then fast dwindling class.

The bogie-less shell of No 191SA rests on its end skirts and fuel tank at Inchicore on Friday 25 June 1993. This loco ran away driverless under suspicious circumstances from Dublin North Wall Yard on Saturday 17 August 1991. It was diverted by observant signalmen into a headshunt at Clonsilla, in the Dublin outer suburbs, where it collided with the buffer stop. Then it suffered a bogie fire, and the scorch marks can still be noted on the running plate. The number suffix 'S' denotes that the locomotive is equipped with Cab Audible Warning Signalling (CAWS), and the suffix 'A' indicated that it was air-braked.

The scrap line at a misty Inchicore on unlucky Friday 13 May 1994, with the remains of five Class A locomotives, from the front: Nos 040/056/013/007 and 033. In the period May/June 1994 thirteen A Class locomotives were scrapped at Inchicore.

Locomotives at Inchicore awaiting their fate on Wednesday 12 July 1995. Residents include Nos 011/121/001 and 055. The last mentioned was spared and moved by road on 8 July 1998 to Hell's Kitchen (hellskitchenmuseum.com), a railway museum and bar in Castlerea, Co Roscommon, where refreshments can be consumed in the former engine room!

No 174 was kept in the twilight zone for quite a time at Inchicore and is pictured here partially cut up on Friday 22 May 1998 with a cutter's torch mark around the cab floor line. It was undergoing bodywork repairs in late 1993 when work was stopped. The locomotive was then cannibalised for spare parts and eventually scrapped together with No 132 on the right, in December 2002. The truncated remains of No 191 (the run-away) pictured on page 172 can be seen on the left.

A rather macabre scene in the running shed at Belfast York Road on Saturday 9 August 1997. A six piece 80 class set comprising vehicles 82-772-737-751-778-93 was hijacked at Bells Row level crossing near Lurgan on 6 July while working the 12.32 from Belfast Central to Portadown. The train was evacuated and petrol bombs placed on board, and later detonated as the train straddled Lake Street level crossing. All the passenger saloons were destroyed, graffiti was daubed on the coach sides while the train sat marooned until the early hours of 8 July when it was removed to Belfast. The four intermediate coach bodies were scrapped at Belfast Harbour estate in October 1997, the bogies were retained as spares. Power cars 82 and 93 were repaired at Railcare in Glasgow, returning to traffic in September and October 1999.

Three MV class locomotives are grounded awaiting the cutters torch in Belfast Harbour estate on Saturday 23 August 1997. Nos 108/105/104 were moved by road for scrapping, less their bogies, which the scrap man dealt with at Fortwilliam storage sidings. No 106 was perhaps more fortunate, leaving Fortwilliam in October 1997 on its long journey by road to Cahirciveen for preservation. The other two members of NIR's MV class of six, 107 and 109 had already been scrapped, 107 along with CIÉ 224 (originally to have been NIR 105) were dealt with at Ballymena in January 1996, 109 was scrapped at York Road works in March 1993.

The locomotive headlamps of 153 and 128 illuminate the rear of Sligo's home signals as they depart with the 18.20 to Dublin Connolly on Tuesday 7 February 1989. The signal man is out on the platform with the electric train staff (ETS) for the section to Ballymote, immediately before departure of this, the last passenger train from Sligo for the day. Further activity later that night was the arrival of the evening passenger train from Connolly at 21.45, and the departure of the Sligo Quay to Dublin North Wall liner at 22.35. The 19.20 liner from the North Wall did not arrive in to Sligo until around 02.30 the following morning, having crossed the 22.35 during its hour and a half wait at Longford.

I used to take a Rail Rambler ticket for a week in February, taking a lot of photographs at night. I often wondered when I would get arrested for lurking in the shadows, but I must say that staff all over the system were always very encouraging towards someone showing an interest in their railway.